D0753977

BISON
BOOKS

Overland in 1835 *Photograph Courtesy of California Historical Society*

Women of the West

DOROTHY GRAY

INTRODUCTION TO THE BISON BOOKS EDITION BY
Paula Mitchell Marks

University of Nebraska Press
Lincoln and London

⊛ The paper in this book meets the minimum requirements of Amereican National
Standard for Information Sciences—Permanence of Paper for Printed Library
Materials, ANSI Z39.48-1984.

First Bison Books printing: 1998
Most recent printing indicated by the last digit below:
10   9   8   7   6   5   4   3   2   1

Library of Congress Cataloging-in-Publication Data
Gray, Dorothy, 1936–
Women of the West / Dorothy Gray; introduction to the Bison Books edition by
Paula Mitchell Marks.
p.   cm.
Originally published: Millbrae, Calif.: Les Femmes, c1976.
Includes bibliographical references and index.
ISBN 0-8032-7073-9 (pa: alk. paper)
1. Women—West (U.S.)—Biography.   I. Title.
HQ1412.G73   1998
920.72′0978—dc21
98-22580   CIP

Reprinted from the original 1976 edition by Les Femmes, Millbrae CA.

To my daughter Michele Kathleen, hard-working young woman who helped her mom and who stands on today's new frontier for women. To my sons Dan, Jeremy, Tim, Matthew and Teddy, whose cooperation and patience made the work possible. To my great-grandmother Sally Shields O'Neil, pioneer who set an example of strength for generations of her family. And to my mother Grace Daley Kamer, who has lived out that example in her own life and carried forward a heritage of hope.

Acknowledgments

Thanks to Phyllis Butler, editor and dear friend, for more than can be expressed. To teachers Ted Tajima, Tony Turhollow, Travis Bogard, Henry Nash Smith, George Stewart, and Marc Schorer, whose standards of excellence and scholarship can scarcely be measured by the performance of their student. To Rosemary, Betty and Carol for heroic typing. To the staffs of the Bancroft Library, California State Library, Cameron House, and Los Altos Library for great assistance. And to a dear companion who shared the love of the West, encouraged me in my work, but for whom trail's end came too soon.

Introduction to the Bison Books Edition

Paula Mitchell Marks

When Les Femmes Press published Dorothy Gray's *Women of the West* in 1976, historians had paid little attention to nineteenth-century western women beyond promulgating the usual "one-dimensional stereotypes" prevalent in popular culture.[1] A rich and exciting American women's history had been developing, spurred in part by the women's rights movement and its adherents' interest in the feminist works of Simone de Beauvoir and Betty Friedan. Yet the path-breaking historians of American women's experience—such theorists as Barbara Welter and Gerda Lerner—had focused overwhelmingly in the late 1960s on the lives of antebellum eastern women. This trend had continued in the early 1970s.[2]

Meanwhile, nineteenth-century western women continued to be depicted as "gentle tamers" (the title of a popular book by Dee Brown first published in 1958 and reprinted in 1968 and 1974), as "madonnas of the prairies," as "Calamity Janes," as clearly secondary or even tangential "helpmates" in the conquest of the American frontier. And minority western women remained virtually invisible, aside from the occasional romanticized or derogatory portrait of Native American women.

In 1976 our understanding had not yet been informed and enhanced by such western women's history scholars as Susan Armitage, Elizabeth Jameson, Julie Roy Jeffrey, Sandra Myers, Paula Petrik, Glenda Riley, and Lillian Schlissel. Nancy Wilson Ross's 1944 *Westward the Women* for decades had stood virtually alone as a challenge to simplistic and peripheral portraits of western frontier women. Western women's history was slowly beginning to percolate with Mary W. M. Hargreaves's early-1970s work on plains women. Then the year 1976 saw the publication both of Christine Stansell's "Women on the Great Plains, 1865–1900" in the fourth issue of *Women's Studies* and of Gray's *Women of the West.*

Glenda Riley identifies Gray's work as one of "a few early dissident voices" raised against "stereotypical depictions" of western women.[3] Indeed, in her depiction of various nineteenth-century western women, Gray developed a number of forward-looking themes.

First, Gray sought to show the ways in which women in the nineteenth-century West actively defined themselves. In other words, she eschewed the passive image of the westering woman in favor of a more complex, more dynamic portrait and did so in part by "go[ing] back to the lives and the writings of the women themselves to find out what it was they truly were." She found tremendous personal determination and courage in such stories as that of Bethenia Owens-Adair, who overcame a disastrous early marriage and strong social resistance to become a physician, and that of Juliet Brier, who proved in one fellow traveler's estimation "the best man of the party" on a hellish trek across western deserts in 1849. She also found tremendous growth in such stories as that of Louise Clappe, who engaged in an "extraordinary movement . . . from the stereotype of feminine frailty to sturdy confidence."

While such conclusions have a clearly celebratory tone, Gray was careful not to lay a positive gloss over lives still bound in large part by stifling convention. Narcissa Whitman remained trapped in "her narrow system of values" in her years at the Walla Walla mission station; her tragedy lay in part in being "thrust into an unsuitable and demanding role by her deep desire to make something significant of her life when there was no suitable channel for her talents." At the same time, Gray pointed out, Whitman demonstrated bravery and persistence.

A second major point that Gray developed was that of the significance of women's accomplishments. Sacajawea was presented as "a major figure at a critical moment of American history," Louise Clappe as the premier chronicler of the gold-rush society that flourished in early California, Willa Cather as "the first writer to transmute the American West and the pioneer experience into major literature."

But Gray also moved beyond recognition of obvious public achievements to appreciation of women's previously unsung contributions within their families and extended communities. "The entire operation of the cattle industry," she noted, "would not have been possible without the ability of women to endure the long absences of their men in an area where the next nearest ranch might be thirty miles away." In observing that Juliet Brier's successful attempt to get her family's cattle to Los Angeles "meant her family would have something of value with which to start life anew," Gray anticipated current understandings of the ways in which frontier women contributed directly to the family's economic welfare.

Gray further extended the scope of western women's history by acknowledging and discussing minority women and some of the added obstacles they faced in a West becoming increasingly indifferent or hostile to their presence. She overgeneralized about the sad state of Indian women within their own cultures, concluding that they uniformly occupied a very lowly place, "often [as] little more than objects of convenience." Yet at least she sought to expose the untenable situations into which they—and Hispanic, African American, and Chinese women—were pushed.

Further, Gray did not fall into the trap of viewing minority women only as passive victims; western women "of whatever race" and whatever the environmental and societal factors were "makers of history" as well as willing or unwilling participants in the unfolding story of the West.

Another way in which Gray sought to push the boundaries of mid-1970s understanding was by recognizing significant regional differences in women's experiences. Specifically, she contrasted western women's lives and opportunities with those of eastern women and found the latter wanting: eastern society "was growing more repressive for women and more constrictive," its upper-class women "kept as petted, mindless darlings," its lower-class women "consigned to . . . mills and sweat shops." The West "offered not only the opportunity but the necessity of being the fullest, strongest, most independent and competent person that any woman or man could be."

We now tend to see more commonality than difference in the experience of women who were part of the dominant nineteenth-century American culture. Contemporary historians note that gender roles remained strong on the frontier, with "resistance tend[ing] to be random and intermittent."[4] Some of the independent growth that Gray celebrated as a result of the frontier experience—for example, the transition from women riding sidesaddle to riding astride and even becoming rodeo champions—reflected the fact that a new generation of women had grown up on the frontier, rather than the idea that the pioneering generation of women had adapted to greater freedoms. One can also argue that by the 1890s growing numbers of women in the East and the South, far from being "petted, mindless darlings," were in the process of redefining and extending their own roles into the public sphere.[5]

Yet Gray's basic points remain sound. Their experiences in the West called forth a real resourcefulness, self-reliance, and, yes, heroism among western women. While they did indeed inhabit gendered roles, most also remained working partners in family and community enterprise based on preindustrial models. Their work days could be back-breaking, but as the consumer culture in the East undercut old patterns of female productivity, the worth of western women's efforts was apparent in a variety of tangible ways—butter on the table, clothes on the family's backs, egg money in a jar, a sick calf healing in the barn. And women often were responsible for the running of farms and ranches for long periods.

In addition, Gray's emphasis on greater possibility and liberty in the West is echoed by many of the women themselves. "The very air I breathe seems so very free that I have not the least desire to return [to Maine]," wrote new Californian Mary Jane Magquier.[6] If women's experience of western freedom was generally more limited and more uneven than men's, many at different times and different places did enjoy a lessening of gender restrictions. Evidence for this conclusion ranges from western courts' affirmation of women's property rights to the freer and easier social relations commented upon by both women and men in many western towns.

Gray expressed the hope in her 1976 introduction that more scholarship using "diaries, journals, and letters of Western women" would be forthcoming. Her hope has been amply realized in the wealth of scholarship now available. But her own work still stands as a valid and valuable testament to the ways in which women met challenges in the developing American West.

NOTES

1. Glenda Riley, in *The Female Frontier: A Comparative View of Women on the Prairie and the Plains* (Lawrence: University Press of Kansas, 1988), states, "Until the mid 1970s, frontierswomen appeared in histories of the American West only as one-dimensional stereotypes or not at all" (1).

2. In an interview conducted by Roger Adelson and published in *The Historian* 60, 1 (fall 1997), prominent American women's historian Mary Beth Norton notes, "U.S. women's history . . . in the early 1970s was concentrated primarily on the antebellum period."

3. Riley, *Female Frontier*, 10 and endnote.

4. Riley, *Female Frontier*, 4.

5. See, for example, Sara M. Evans's *Born for Liberty: A History of Women in America* (New York: Free Press, 1989).

6. Qtd. in Paula Mitchell Marks, *Precious Dust: The American Gold Rush Era: 1848–1900* (New York: William Morrow & Company, 1994; Lincoln: University of Nebraska Press, 1998), 364.

Contents

When I stop at one of the graveyards in my own county. . .
I have always the hope that something went into the ground
with those pioneers that will one day come out again.
Something that will come out not only in sturdy traits of character,
but in elasticity of mind,
in an honest attitude toward the realities of life,
in certain qualities of feeling and imagination.

— Willa Cather

Introduction

Like a great natural line of demarcation the Mississippi River divided America in two. Beyond its waters lay the West, a vast and complex land so different in its nature that the experience there was totally different than it had been for those who had pioneered east of the river. The West was vast and open of aspect, semi-arid, almost treeless, cut by huge mountain ranges. On a clear day you really could see forever. It was the land of the big sky, of the wide open spaces.

For many who pioneered there it was an exhilarating experience. But it was also a harsh and strange land. The weather and sub-climates were extreme, ranging from desert to high blizzard country. Flood, earthquake, drought, prairie fire, tornado—disaster was commonplace. There was no previous American experience that could entirely prepare people for the impact of the West. Even to describe it, Americans had to borrow from other languages: *arroyo, canyon, mesa, prairie.* Some people took a look at the West and turned back, finding it frighteningly strange after their Eastern homes of gentle wooded, well-watered land.

The Western experience was thus set in a spectacular, alien land. It is hard now to recapture in our own feelings how truly strange it was to the American pioneers. All over the world in recent generations people have become accustomed to the images of the West through the countless motion pictures filmed there. There are few places so remote in this world that its inhabitants have not seen cowboys galloping across the vivid landscape of the American West. Mesa, mountain, sand dune, gulch and gully are now known everywhere and are

1

probably a more familiar and comfortable part of the interior landscape of the American psyche than is the urban or suburban landscape of our actual lives.

But in the beginning the land was not comfortable psychologically; only the strongest and most adaptable could become at home there.

The Western experience was strange not only in terms of the physical place but also in terms of time. The Mississippi River was not only a physical demarcation but also a time belt. By mid-19th century, east of the river America was moving into the Industrial Age and the Victorian era. Petty conventions and restrictive customs were enveloping the East just at the time that the most free and wildly individualistic era of American history was beginning west of the river. People who crossed the river went physically from one world to another. The tumultuous changes taking place both East and West were pulling in opposite directions and this difference of direction was particularly dramatic for women.

As Eastern society was growing more repressive for women and more constrictive of their being, the West offered not only the opportunity but the necessity of being the fullest, strongest, most independent and competent person that any woman or man could be. The adventure for women was not only one of physical survival but of psychological growth and gain that can scarcely be over valued when compared with the dismal grey of Victorianism that was falling across the East like a long twilight.

We are accustomed to think of progress as a steady, inevitable thing that builds upon the gains of the past in reliable way. But progress for women in achieving full potential has been an uneven thing. The sad truth is that women were further ahead in the time of George Washington than they were in the time of Abraham Lincoln. Abigail Adams could write to her husband John Adams and request forthrightly that women be given the vote under the new constitution. It was not a low opinion of women that kept them from voting status in the new republic so much as it was the habit of English law; women, generally speaking, were well-regarded in early America. Foreigners commonly expressed surprise at the respect accorded the female, at the generally high level of education and conversation among American women, and at their overall sense of competency and significance.

The Victorian Age and the Industrial Revolution debased women. Labor-saving devices, canned foods, store bought goods—all eroded their significance in family survival. Men left the home and farm and went to work in factories, and women were left behind to fill their days with "genteel arts" that amounted to little more than paper doll cutting. Man and woman were no longer partners in work and survival. He was the paid laborer, she the kept and fragile female child. Woman in America, beginning around 1840, took a long step backward from her colonial grandmother.

The West was different. Here women were scarce, valuable, and valued. They were not valued as decorative objects but for their real skills and their true sexuality. Ironically, because they were truly valuable, they were not pampered as were their Eastern sisters. The legendary gallantry of the West was tempered by hard realism. A cowboy might punch a man who insulted even a prostitute but a woman might also have to shoot her own food or for her own protection. The West was fair. Those who had to pull their own weight became independent, reached for their full rights and got them.

Progress is indeed not steady. The women of the West did not triumph as the prevailing model for American woman. The West was far removed from the centers that influenced American thought and mores. American publishing was centered in the East and the images of American women that permeated American thought until the close of the 19th century were Eastern. When Western woman was portrayed in popular literature or periodicals it was in her most sensationalized form: Calamity Jane, Belle Starr and the prostitute with heart of gold or, in contrast, the long-suffering and essentially passive pioneer woman in sunbonnet who endured much but contributed little other than to have "civilized" the West by the somehow holy and sentimentalized fact of her womanhood.

Each was a shallow and skewered view of Western woman and one that has, unfortunately, prevailed into our own time. Almost alone in literature Willa Cather tried to convey in her fiction the fuller range of Western woman. Other writers, mostly male, have stuck with too narrow an image whether in fiction or popular studies. One must go back to the lives and the writings of the women themselves to find what it was they truly were—such is attempted in this book.

I have also tried to include a feeling of what the Western experience was for minority women. They were not subject to the Victorianization of white Eastern women but to social conditioning of other kinds. Native American society was, until the advent of whites, rigidly structured. The Indian woman's place was secure but closely defined, almost approaching chattel status. The tumultuous changes in the West both destroyed and liberated them. Black women who had experienced slavery had never known pampering and were perhaps, like Biddy

Mason, more physically and emotionally fit for the independence of the West, but they were, as were all women of color, also more subject to the explosive violence or persistent exploitation of women in a lawless land. Like Indian women, Mexican-American women saw their society destroyed by the onslaught of Yankees. Chinese women were often enslaved to satisfy the rampant love of pleasure that was even then a falsely glorified part of the Western tradition.

But women of the West of whatever race were not uniformly victims of either the environment or the society around them. They were a part of history but they were also makers of history. They left their names upon the land and upon literature. They helped, as is notable in the story of Sacajawea, to turn the course of history.

But most of all they made a women's history for those who would follow them. It is a history long neglected and one that perhaps can be appreciated only in our own time when women are exploring once again the frontiers of their own being.

This book does not pretend to be a definitive study of the history or significance of the Western woman. It is an attempt to break trail into that land and time now as far from us as the Far West was then from the settled East. The author sincerely hopes that as more diaries, journals, and letters of Western women come to light, more will be written of those who pioneered so bravely in so many ways and who triumphed in the only ways that are truly lasting and significant, the triumph of self and strength.

1

Sacajawea

The Shadows of History

The Indian woman to whom I ascribe equal fortitude and resolution . . .
The Journal of Meriwether Lewis,
May 16, 1805

Across the West more memorials of various kinds commemorate Sacajawea than any other woman in American history. Her name is to be found on everything from mountains and lakes to museums and Girl Scout camps.

So widely has she become a legend of romantic nature for her role in the Lewis and Clark expedition that the true facts of her life and the true significance of her story have been almost entirely obscured—the actual Sacajawea has remained a figure hidden in the shadows of history. Since she could neither read nor write nor speak any of the white man's languages she left no first-hand record of her life or feelings. What we know of her is contained in the often brief journal entries of the two captains of the expedition and various other members of the party.

Sparce as the record is, however, it establishes Sacajawea as a major figure at a critical moment of American history. At the key moment of crisis in the Lewis and Clark expedition it was upon her that the success of the journey rested and with it the future of the young United States and the dreams of its visionary president, Thomas Jefferson.

Sacajawea not only made a significant contribution to the development of the nation; she did so as an Indian woman. In this latter aspect she is a figure of transition, marking out the sorrows, benefits, and cruel choices that women of various races would experience in the long social upheaval known as the opening of the West.

She was born a Shoshone in about 1789, a member of a subtribe later to be called the Lemhi, who were then living in what is today

5

Idaho. Through acquisition of horses introduced by the Spanish far to the south, the Shoshone group to which she belonged had transformed itself within a generation from a desert tribe living a meager and circumscribed existence in the Great Basin west of the Rockies to being a tribe capable of crossing the splendid heights of the Rocky Mountains to hunt buffalo on the Great Plains to the east.

Another basic change occurred in the life of the tribe shortly after Sacajawea's birth. To the east and north of the Lemhi-Shoshone hunting grounds their implacable foe, the Blackfeet, had obtained guns from the English and French in Canada and were now able to inflict terrible losses upon the Shoshone. Steadily the Shoshone advantage in being mounted was overcome by the Blackfeet's superior weaponry. The Blackfeet were able to drive them from the plains and back into the Rockies, not only securing the hunting area but obtaining Shoshone horses.

So it was that in one lifetime the Lemhis went from being a food-gathering tribe then to being buffalo-hunting Indians and finally to being virtually locked in the game-sparse heights of the Rockies. When Sacajawea was ten or eleven years old her tribe could venture down on the plains after buffalo only at the risk of attack.

On one occasion a war party of Hidatsa Indians, allies of the Blackfeet, surprised the Shoshones at a camp near Three Forks on the Missouri River. At the sound of gunfire the men leapt to their horses and fled, leaving the women, children, and elderly to run towards the woods. A number of Shoshone men and boys were killed, and the attackers rounded up some of the women and children as captives. Sacajawea was taken as she attempted to cross the river at a shallow place.

Now began five long years of exile. Indian captives were generally regarded as slaves, however it is unlikely that Sacajawea or the other children were mistreated since Indians were usually gentle with children. The difficult part was separation from homeland and family. Rather than endure such separation, a number of the children risked escape and a long dangerous journey home through hundreds of miles of strange land. It is not factually known why Sacajawea did not join them, but tradition says she chose to stay with a young friend, Otter Woman, who could not be roused from sleep the night of the escape.

Sacajawea and the other captives of the Hidatsa were taken to Mandan Indian villages on· the upper Missouri River near today's Bismarck, North Dakota. It was a tremendous change; from this place on the vast flat plains the Shoshones could not even see the soaring mountains that had been their home.

But there were other changes of even greater significance. Sacajawea was now brought into contact with one of the most developed and admirable people among the Western Indians. The Mandans were a permanently settled tribe, living in earthen lodges and engaged in farming. They were an unusually handsome people, tall and of fine

form, and noted for their intelligence and level dispositions. Among
the plains Indians they were the only people who made pottery.

Here at the cluster of five villages on the Missouri were encamped
over 4,000 Mandans and the related Arikaras and Hidatsas, the largest
single concentration of Indians west of the Mississippi. The villages
formed an important trade center to which came Indians from a wide
area of the West to trade. Through here passed beaver and otter pelts,
deerskins, hides of elk and even white buffalo, beads of bone,
ornaments of shells and feathers, and, increasingly, white people's
goods. By this time the French and English traders from Canada had
worked their way up the Missouri seeking precious furs.

For a young Indian girl from the fastness of the Rockies the life at
the Mandan villages must have been an incredible spectacle of change
and novelty. Even the Cheyenne came to trade for Mandan corn, an
item they still relished from the days before they were driven into a
nomadic life from their Minnesota farms by eastern tribes. At this point
in time there was in process tremendous displacement of tribes
throughout the country in a far-reaching domino effect, and the
Mandan villages were virtually in the center of the flux. White traders
were attracted by the ready access to immense trade opportunities at
the villages as well as by the fact that the Mandans liked whites and
welcomed them. (Within a few years the Mandans were totally wiped
from the face of the earth by the whites' diseases.)

It was at the Mandan villages that Sacajawea and Otter Woman grew
to what was then considered womanhood by both Indians and whites.
And at about age fifteen Sacajawea and her slightly older companion
were either bartered or gambled away by their Hidatsa master to a
Frenchman named Touissant Charbonnier who took the two girls as
wives. This degrading treatment was not an uncommon occurrence on
the frontier and among the Indian tribes themselves women were often
little more than objects of convenience. In fairness, however, there
were Indian men who deeply loved their wives as did some of the
lonely white men who took Indian wives and provided for them as well
as they could in the uncertain conditions of the frontier.

There is no way to know how Sacajawea regarded her marriage to
Charbonnier. The fact that it was polygamous undoubtedly mattered
little since in many tribes sisters or good friends rejoiced in being
married to the same man. As for Charbonnier himself, he had lived
among the Mandan and other tribes for almost a decade and thus must
have been held in fairly good repute by them, which would have
counted in his favor with his Indian wives.

For an Indian woman marriage to a white man offered the possibility of enjoying the highly prized white men's goods and could mean a somewhat easier if less secure life than marriage within the tribe offered. For Indian women marrying whites at this time, there was often not even a question of separation from the tribe or alienation from their own culture since the white traders or trappers often entered into the life of the tribe.

In the autumn of 1804 a new element was introduced into the life at the Mandan villages. A large party of Americans arrived. Known as the Corps of Discovery, it was headed by Captains Meriwether Lewis and William Clark, under direction from President Thomas Jefferson to explore through to the Pacific Ocean. The expedition leaders decided to winter over at the villages and set about building Fort Mandan.

On November 4 Charbonnier came in from a hunt on the plains and applied to the expedition for a job as an interpreter. A week later Sacajawea appeared at the fort with Otter Woman, recorded in Clark's journal in his individualistic spelling.

> (November 11, 1804)
> Continued at work at the fort Two men cut themselves with an ax, The large Ducks pass to the South an Indian gave me several roles of parched meat two Squars of the Rock(y) mountains, purchased from the Indians by a frenchman came down The Mandans out hunting Buffalow . . .

Sacajawea was singularly unimportant to Clark at this point, rating somewhere below rolls of jerked meat and the flight of migrating fowl. To some of the Indians at the fort however, those who had been far to the west, Clark gave full attention. From them he was piecing together the geography of the land beyond Fort Mandan, a place where no known white had ever gone.

Clark was highly proficient at geography and was able to assemble what would prove to be a highly accurate idea of the territory up to the base of the Rockies. But there his efforts were stalled. Not one among the Indians that he talked to had ever been into these "Shineing Mountains," as he called them. For some reason Clark apparently did not interview the two "Squars of the Rock mountains" who might have been able to fill in some of the great blank space on his map.

During the winter Charbonnier moved into the fort with his two Shoshone wives and possibly a third unnamed Mandan wife. Sacajawea was pregnant and so was Otter Woman, who was already the mother of a young child.

By Christmas the fierce plains winter had driven temperatures to twenty below zero on the thermometer of the Corps of Discovery but the Americans celebrated anyway. One of the privates of the quasi-military expedition wrote:

> At half past two another gun was fired, as a notice to assemble at the dance, which was continued in a jovial manner till eight at night; and without the presence of any females except three squaws, wives to our interpreter, who took no part other than the amusement of looking on.

Even with the novel ways of Americans to observe, it still must have been a rather confined life for the Indian women that winter at the fort. Lewis discovered that they were opening the gate of the fort to Indian friends late at night, and he ordered a lock to be put upon the gate.

Then in January Clark learned something that made the Shoshone, Sacajawea, a potentially significant asset to the expedition. A war chief from the Gros Ventres tribe revealed to Clark his plan to attack the Shoshones in the spring. The last thing that Clark wanted was war upon the plains the Corps would be crossing, and he dissuaded the young chief. But from the conversation Clark learned that the Shoshones had horses. Lewis and Clark had some idea that an overland journey might be necessary in the Rockies between the headwaters of the Missouri River and the beginning of a navigable river flowing to the Pacific. Although they thought such a portage would only be a day or two in duration, the availability of horses must certainly have seemed a potential advantage. It is quite likely that at this point they surmised that Sacajawea could be of help in securing horses from her people. Her presence was of far greater importance than they could have known at the time.

Lewis and Clark had other matters to consider that winter. From the English and French traders who came to the fort, the captains learned that two English fur companies in Canada had merged and would soon be able to move into the unclaimed lands of the far northwest along the Columbia River and even further south. If that occurred before the Americans lay claim through exploration, then President Jefferson's dream of one nation spanning a continent would be foreclosed forever. Clearly Lewis and Clark were in a race with the British and history.

As the winter dragged on, the men were impatient to be under way. Clark planned for the expedition to move out as soon as the ice broke on the Missouri. But winter kept a tight grip. On January 6 Clark wrote of "a verry fine worm Day," but on February 3, Lewis complained that "the situation of our boat and pirogues is now allarming, they are firmly inclosed in the Ice and almost covered with Snow.''

Meantime, Sacajawea awaited the birth of her baby. If the baby was not born before the ice broke, she would be left behind. Then, on February 11, Lewis made the following entry in his journal:

> about five oClock this evening one of the wives of Charbobo was delivered of a fine boy, it is worth of remark that this is the first child which this woman had boarn, and as is common in such cases her labour was tedious and the pain violent; Mr. Jessome informed me that he had frequently administered a small portion of the rattle of the rattlesnake, which he assured me had never failed to produce the desired effect, that of hastening the birth of the child; having the rattle of a snake by me I gave it to him and he administered two rings of it to the woman broken in small pieces with the fingers and added to a small quantity of water. Whether this medicine was truly the cause or not I shall not undertake to determine, but I was informed that she had not taken it more than ten minutes before she brought forth.

The baby was officially named Jean Baptiste, but Sacajawea called him Pomp, a name in Shoshone meaning first born or leader of men.

Less than two weeks later the ice had begun to loosen and the men were able to free the boats; preparations for departure began.

Most of the month of March was taken up with preparing the boats and loading in supplies. In mid-March Charbonnier suddenly decided to back out of the expedition rather than commit himself to a contract that might call for hard physical work. Two days later, Charbonnier changed his mind again and sent an intermediary to say that he was very sorry "for the foolish part he had acted" and that he would very much like to accompany the expedition. It was by such a narrow margin that history was determined, for had Charbonnier not gone the expedition would have been deprived of the help of Sacajawea at its most critical moment.

On March 24 Clark "saw Swans and Wild Gees flying N.E." On the next day he reported "the ice began to break away." Spring had come and it was time to go forward.

Sacajawea undoubtedly understood that the Corps of Discovery was headed for her home and possible reunion with her tribe. But she was now to be parted from Otter Woman by order of the captains who ruled that the latter could not go on the trip. Otter Woman was expecting another child and the expedition could not risk the certainty of a birth upon the trail. Tradition says that the two Shoshone women wept upon being parted.

Representatives of the powerful English fur companies hung around until the last, hopeful of going with the Americans. But Lewis and Clark were too shrewd to allow a joint exploration and the possible confusion of claims that could follow.

The departure day was April 7, 1805, and Lewis wrote eloquently of the prospects before them.

> Our vessels consisted of six small canoes and two large pirogues. This little fleet altho' not quite so rispectable as those of Columbus or Capt. Cook, were still viewed by us with as much pleasure as those deservedly famed adventurers ever beheld theirs; and I dare say with quite as much anxiety for their safety and preservation. we were now about to penetrate a country at least two thousand miles in width, on which the foot of civilized man had never trodden . . . I could but esteem this moment of my departure as among the most happy of my life. The party are in excellent health and sperits, zealously attached to enterprise and anxious to proceed. . . .

Clark too wrote of the departure, but he confined his journal entry principally to a rollcall of the party.

> our party consisting of Sergts. Nathaniel Pryor, John Ordway, Patrick Gass. Pvts. William Bratton, John Colter, Joseph and Reuben Fields, John Shields, George Gibson, George Shannon, John Potts, John Collins, Joseph Whitehouse, Richard Windsor, Alexander Willard, Hugh Hall, Silas Goodrich, Robert Frazier, Peter Cruzatte, Baptiste Lepage, Francis Labiche, Hugh McNeal, William Werner, Thomas P. Howard, Peter Wiser, John B. Thompson, and my servant York, George Drewyer who acts as a hunter and interpreter, Charbonneau and his Indian Squar to act as an Interpreter and Interpretess for the snake Indians—one Mandan & Charbonneau's infant.

Thus had Sacajawea, a nameless "squar," become a properly titled person with a recognized position.

Of the others in the party, the leaders were far and away the most remarkable. Captain Meriwether Lewis, age thirty, a former aide of Thomas Jefferson's, was a man of immense frontier experience. He was of serious mind and purpose, reserved in manner, and singularly adept at managing his men and the Indians they encountered. Further, much of the careful observation of flora and fauna, Indian life, and geological features so meticulously recorded by the expedition was the work of Lewis.

Clark, a few years older, was something of a contrast in personality, a gregarious redhead, open and affable of nature. Like Lewis he had considerable frontier and military experience. He also had a remarkable gift for geography and it was generally he who was pilot on the trip.

Almost from the first Sacajawea was useful to the Corps of Discovery as Lewis noted with the same careful attention he gave to recording all observations of new customs and other phenomenon.

> Tuesday, April 9
> when we halted for dinner the squaw busied herself in serching for the wild artichokes which mice collect and deposit in hoards. this operation she performed by penetrating the earth with a sharp stick about some small collection of drift wood. her labour soon proved successful and she procured a good quantity of these roots. the flavor of this root resembles that of the Jerusalem Artichoke, and the stalk of the weed which produces it is also similar.

As the journey up the Missouri progressed, there was much hard work getting the boats upstream against the strong current, but the country was full of the wonders of a new land unseen before by whites and unsullied by their ways. The Corps was passing through a paradise that all too soon would be lost. Lewis and Clark each took note of the scene through which they were passing.

> great numbers of brant flying up the river, the Maple and Elm had buded and cotton and arrow wood beginning to bud . . .
> Saw Great numbers of gees feedin in the Praries on the young grass, I saw flowers in the praries to day . . .
> where the land is level it is uniformly fertile . . . very much blue grass . . .
> the game such as Buffalow, Elk, antelopes, and Deer verry plenty . . .
> saw some plumb bushes in full bloom, The beaver of this river is much larger than usial . . .
> immence herds of Buffaloe, Elk, deer, & Antelopes feeding in one common and boundless pasture . . .

The abundant wildlife included astonishing numbers of huge grizzly bears that constantly menaced the party. Rattlesnakes too were a hazard, and the black flies and "musquetors" were a ceaseless nuisance to everyone. No mention is made of any complaint by Sacajawea so we can assume that she literally took all in stride, no mean accomplishment with a young baby to care for; even the Indians rarely undertook such long treks with women and small children.

During this part of the journey an incident occurred that revealed a great deal of the inner fibre of the woman. The event also discredits arguments that she had no understanding of the importance or meaning of the journey. On May 14 Lewis and Clark were both walking on shore, a rare occurrence. Suddenly a squall of wind struck and the main boat began to tip alarmingly to one side. Charbonnier was at the helm and, not being a swimmer, was seized with panic. Helpless from their position on the banks, Lewis and Clark watched horrified as the boat went "topsaturva" and water rushed over the side, threatening the lives of the best of their crewmen and Sacajawea and her baby. For Lewis the expedition itself was sinking; "in this perogue were embarked our papers, Instruments, books, medicines, a great part of our merchandise and in short almost every article indispensibly necessary to . . . insure the success of the enterprize in which we were now launched to the distance of 2200 miles."

Only when another crewman trained his gun on him did Charbonnier contain his panic and take proper measures to right the boat while the others frantically bailed. Of all the people in the imperiled boat it was Sacajawea, with drowning an imminent threat to her and the baby on her back, who calmly reached out and grabbed the precious articles that were being washed overboard.

In Lewis' next journal entry, when he had somewhat shaken the horror of the near disaster, he acknowledged her actions and commended "her equal fortitude and resolution." Within the week the party named a river for her, marking the first time that her name appeared in the journals.

Although Lewis remarked her usefulness, generally it was Clark who seems to have been more warm and friendly. Early on it became his habit to walk with the Charbonnier family along the banks of the river. Tradition has attempted to romanticize the relationship between Sacajawea and Clark but there is no evidence that they were in love with one another. In fact, not long after the naming of the Sacajawea River, Clark named the Judith River for a young woman back in Virginia whom he married when the expedition returned home. What special feeling there might have been between the two travelers was most likely centered on Clark's love for the baby, Pomp. Clark was himself from a large family and throughout his life he showed a great fondness and concern for children. Over the long journey the Indian infant became for Clark, "my Pomp."

As May passed into June, the journey became more arduous. The men labored in icy water up to their shoulders to keep the boats moving past obstacles and riffles or strained at tow ropes to work the boats upstream. Illness and accidents occurred close in succession: fevers, dysentery, carbuncles, sprains. The weather of the high plains inflicted its sudden changes, its cold nights and burning days.

At last they reached the long sought Great Falls of the Missouri. It was an important achievement, confirming to the leaders that thus far they had correctly charted their course. But joy soon faded in the face of hardship. For a full month they labored to get their canoes and equipment up the falls. At one place the ground was covered with cactus and the spines cruelly pierced their feet through their mocassins.

Sadly, they suffered more than was necessary. The slow ordeal round the falls was rooted in the persistent dream of the Northwest Passage sought by explorers since the time of Columbus. They were sure that somewhere, only a day's portage beyond this river, there would be navigable waters to carry them to the Western sea.

Halfway through the ordeal at the Great Falls Sacajawea fell ill. Lewis and Clark took turns doctoring her, and their journals reflect their anxiety as she lay near death in the stern of the boat. Lewis took sick with the same ailment, probably intestinal flu, but it was Sacajawea who seemed beyond saving. The two men tried all the remedies of the times: bleedings, poultices, laudanum. Finally, Lewis gave her a drink from an odorous sulphur spring and proudly reported that she began almost immediately to recover. (Today this spring is posted as unfit for human consumption.)

Not long after her recovery, however, Sacajawea had another close brush with death. Along with Clark and Charbonnier, she and her baby took shelter in a gully during a sudden storm. Without warning a flash flood roared down upon them. Clark grabbed Sacajawea and her child and pushed them up the canyon wall. They escaped seconds ahead of the fifteen foot wall of water.

On July 4 the Great Falls were surmounted and a celebration was held. But the hard work was by no means over. Even though the river course leveled out somewhat beyond the falls, the ascent against the current was still difficult. Almost another month passed as they worked their way up into the Rockies to the place called Three Forks. Here, at a crossroads for Indian travel from all over the west, the Missouri divided and the Corps of Discovery elected to take the branch that they named for Jefferson. By this time the heavy work was taking its toll. Charbonnier, oldest of the group at forty-six, was almost played out and "one of his ankles (was) falling him." Clark took very ill with chills and fever and "aking pains in all his bones." Others of the party suffered various complaints.

Yet there was reason to hope. On July 28 Sacajawea recognized familiar territory, the place where the Hidatsa had fallen upon her tribe and carried her off years ago. Strangely enough, in all the journeying from Fort Mandan the party had encountered no Indians, and by now Lewis was seriously worried.

> we begin to feel considerable anxiety with rispect to the Snake Indians. if we do not find them or some other nation who have horses I fear the successfull issue of our voyage will be very doubtful . . . we are now several hundred miles within the bosom of this wild and mountainous country, where game may rationally be expected shortly to become scarce and subsistence precarious without any information with rispect to the country not knowing how far these mountains continue . . .

If they were to proceed over the mountains they must have horses soon. They had reached the point at which the expedition must decide to continue or turn back.

At this most critical moment Sacajawea again sighted familiar terrain and announced that they were near the home of her people. With this encouragement Lewis determined to push ahead and find the Shoshones. He picked out the least lame of his crew (Shields, McNeal and Drewyer) and set off, leaving the main body to push along as best it could under Clark's direction. As helpful as she might have been, Sacajawea was left with Clark. Lewis did not believe that Carbonnier's ankle was healed and apparently did not want to risk bad feelings by separating the husband and wife.

As Lewis went ahead the entire hope of the expedition rested upon making contact with the Shoshones. Four months had passed since leaving Fort Mandan and if the Indians were not found soon the party would have to turn back or risk being trapped by an early winter. By this time Lewis had begun to suspect that the Northwest Passage by water from ocean to ocean was only a dream and that a long overland journey would be necessary. More than ever the need for horses was critical.

Finally, on August 11, Lewis saw in the distance a mounted Indian. He tried to signal the man to come closer but the Indian fled in fear. Lewis and his men followed. In doing so they passed a narrow valley between high peaks and thus, on August 12, 1805, they crossed the Continental Divide, the first Americans to do so.

Lewis knelt down and drank from a tiny, clear mountain stream flowing westward, rejoicing that he had drunk from the headwaters of the mighty Columbia River he had sought so long. The shallow mountain stream was not the Columbia but only a distant tributary.

Nevertheless Lewis' moment of triumph in crossing the divide was real enough.

The next day they came upon more Indians but these too fled. At last they found an old Indian woman and a little girl who, despairing of flight, sat with bowed heads as though awaiting a death blow from the strangers. Lewis put down his gun and approached them. He raised them up and then gave them presents and painted their faces with vermillion as a symbol of peace. Their relief could only have been second to his at finally finding the elusive Shoshones.

Before long he and his men were in the midst of the tribe, being embraced and smeared with bear grease and paint until Lewis was "heartily tired of the national hug." The exuberant welcome was short-lived, however. As soon as Lewis proposed that the Shoshones return with him to the main body of the expedition the Indians grew suspicious that the white men were luring them into a trap set by their mortal enemies, the Blackfeet. Lewis finally persuaded them to accompany him to the rendezvous with Clark, but when they arrived at the designated spot Clark was not there and the Indians' suspicions returned.

Lewis was frantic that he might lose contact with the Shoshones and in his anxiety he resorted to minor trickery. On his advance trip he had attached a note for Clark to a tree at the rendezvous and now, in view of the Indians, he removed the note, read it, and announced that it was from his friend, saying that he would arrive shortly. The ruse kept the Indians at the rendezvous but Lewis noted that some of the tribe were still "much dissatisfied." For his part, Lewis spent a near-sleepless night.

The next day the climactic moment came. While Lewis held the Indians at the rendezvous, Clark slowly struggled closer to the meeting place. Suddenly, he saw Sacajawea ahead of the party begin to dance and "show every mark of extravagant joy." She had sighted several Indians on horseback and recognized them as being of her tribe.

> We soon drew to the camp and just as we approached it a woman made her way through the crowd toward Sacajawea, and recognising each other, they embraced with the most tender affection . . . They had been companions in childhood, in the war with the Minnetarees (Hidatsa) they had both been taken prisoners in the same battle, they had shared and softened the rigours of the captivity till one of them escaped from the Minneatarees with scarce a hope of ever seeing her friend relieved from the hands of her enemies.

What happened next was even more incredible. In one of those coincidences that no fiction writer would dare construct, Sacajawea discovered that the chief of the tribe was none other than her own brother. "She instantly jumped up, and ran and embraced him, throwing over him her blanket and weeping profusely." The chief, Cameahwait, was the sole surviving member of her family except for one other brother then absent from the tribe and an orphaned nephew who, states the record, "was immediately adopted by her."

Although the tremendous benefit of the remarkable meeting to the Lewis and Clark expedition was clearly enormous, there is another aspect to the event that is often overlooked—its meaning to Sacajawea. After years of separation from her family, her culture, and her homeland, she had now returned after a long and arduous journey. The most natural thing in the world would have been for her to have chosen to stay with the Lemhis and, indeed, her decision to adopt her orphaned nephew indicates she at first decided to stay.

Yet, in the days that followed she chose another course. She learned that her brother, Chief Cameahwait, had no intention of providing horses and guides as he had promised. So short of food was his tribe that he had decided to leave immediately on a hunting trip, thus stranding the expedition. Sacajawea elected to tell Lewis and Clark that Cameahwait was backing down on his commitment. In betraying what must have been her brother's confidence she severed the tie with her own people completely and threw in her lot with the white men.

The reason seems to lie plainly in the action itself: she cared that the expedition succeed. Somehow across the barriers of language and culture she apparently understood the momentous importance of the trip and with the equal fortitude and resolution she had shown in saving the precious instruments on the Missouri River, she seems to have determined that she would do her part to advance the success of the Corps of Discovery.

Her action enabled Clark to persuade Cameahwait at the last moment to postpone the hunt and provide the horses and guides necessary to continue on across the Rockies. Following a long and difficult overland trip they finally reached the Clearwater River, a tributary of the Columbia that flowed toward the distant sea. Two months later as they neared the Pacific Ocean, "Ocian in view!" wrote Clark. "O! the joy!"

The high point of the great adventure was past. There yet remained a long wet winter camped at the mouth of the Columbia River and the prospect of the long trip back. But the most remarkable part of the journey was done.

At this point an incident occurred in which Sacajawea emerges from the pages of the journals so completely human that it must be noted. A report came to the camp on the Columbia of a whale washed up on the ocean beach. A party was made up to go and see this wonder. "Charbono and his Indian woman were also of this party; the Indian woman was very impo(r)tunate to be permitted to go . . . she observed that she had traveled a long way with us to see the great waters, and that now that this monstrous fish was also to be seen, she thought it very hard she could not be permitted to see either." Needless to say, Sacajawea saw both ocean and whale. She had indeed traveled a long way.

Although Sacajawea can be seen as a figure symbolic of transition, she represents much more. Through her crucial role in the success of the Corps of Discovery the history of the West and of America was greatly affected.

First and foremost, the successful crossing established firm grounds for America's claim to the far northwest as opposed to that of the British. In the face of British arguments, the expedition was the strong lynchpin that secured the outline of the American nation and opened the territory to the vast migration in the century ahead. Secondly, the expedition literally began the recorded history of the West. Lewis' voluminous notebooks constitute a great scientific record not yet fully appreciated and bear witness to one of the principle purposes of the expedition dear to Jefferson: the increase of knowledge through exploration and scientific observation.

Jefferson had also hoped to establish peace among the Indian tribes within the new territory. In that Lewis and Clark had only temporary success, a brief moment of calm in a long history of inter-tribal warfare. The tremendous territorial struggles as well as the raiding and enslaving of captives had gone on for centuries. A mark of the achievement of Lewis and Clark and Sacajawea is that they entered into territories where inter-tribal hostilities threatened their lives and emerged safely.

Although those who make history affect the course of events, such people are also affected by history. Deep currents of history carried the members of the Corps of Discovery as surely as the currents of the wide Missouri carried their boats.

Among the Corps Sacajawea exemplified more than any other of the party the currents of change in the West. Being female, she would have had little choice of her role in her own tribe had she not been kidnapped and subsequently sold to a white man. Among her own people her life would have been one of simple drudgery, chattel status, and a continuous sameness of existence. With Charbonnier and the white men, her status was markedly improved. She was in time a highly valued member of the expedition and was given the opportunity to emerge from the facelessness of tribal existence to being an individual. Life suddenly extended its horizons, not only to the far Pacific Ocean, but to the experiencing of other cultures. Nevertheless the choice she made to leave her own people was a hard one and the courage that it demanded was no less than the physical courage she demonstrated throughout the journey.

And what of Sacajawea's future when the journey was done? Clark settled a portion of land upon her and Charbonnier in the vicinity of St. Louis and offered to provide for the education of Pomp. After a short while, Charbonnier and Sacajawea tired of farming and returned west, leaving their young boy with Clark to be educated. On December 20, 1812, and at Fort Manuel, located on the present line between North and South Dakota, the clerk of the fort noted the death of "the wife of Charbonneau, a Snake squaw," whom he termed "the best woman in the fort."

Although this and other written evidence indicates that she died at about age thirty, a strong tradition grew up among the Indians that she lived to a great old age and, in the best manner of legends, kept traveling, spending time with tribes from California to Kansas before returning at last to finish her days among her own people. Comanche, Ute, Apache, Shoshone and other tribes—all claim she was with them. Thus have the Indians honored her memory from the beginning. A marker on her alleged burial site can be seen on the Wind River Shoshone Reservation in Wyoming. (Her probable grave site near Fort Manuel has never been located.)

Recognition among whites was slower to come. The flood of books, monuments, and place names honoring Sacajawea did not really begin until near the close of the 19th century.

For Sacajawea the legends and the honors all came too late. Any gratification she may have had must have come from the great adventure and her part in it. She traveled far and she traveled well and she saw a sweep of continent no one had ever seen before.

2

Narcissa Whitman

Overland to the Oregon Territory

Can I leave you, far in heathen lands to dwell?
From hymn sung by
Narcissa Whitman on leaving
her Eastern home

No sooner had Lewis and Clark completed their historic crossing than others followed them into the Far West. On the return trip the explorers encountered two lone men in the vicinity of Yellowstone, the reckless vanguard of hundreds of mountain men who were to explore the vast area over the next decades.

For the next thirty years these mountain men scoured the Western mountains for beaver, trapping every likely river and stream for pelt. An incredible lot, enduring all manner of hardships and danger, they fought and drank hard, and they left their names on the Western land. Some lived with the Indians and adapted totally to their ways; many died in the unending skirmishes between Indian tribes. It was a wild life, culminating each year in a rendezvous held in a chosen mountain valley where "Taos lightning" fueled bloody fights and general hell-raising. This was a strictly male era, the only women occasionally present being those Indian wives who most of the time were left with their tribes while the mountain men each year pushed farther and farther West in the pursuit of the valuable furs.

Then in 1836 the era ended, its closing marked by the passing of the beaver into near-extinction as the meager catch of that year made plain. So heavily had the animal been trapped that the enterprise was no longer economically worthwhile. But the end was marked that year in an even more dramatic way. At the annual rendezvous on the Green River arrived a party of missionaries and their wives bound for Oregon territory. The age of settlement was opening and the wild free days would soon draw to a close.

21

Narcissa Whitman *Photograph Courtesy of Whitman College*

There was undoubtedly some consternation among the mountain men as they beheld white women entering upon the Western scene. White women meant settlements and civilization which over the long course of time would change the face of the country. The settlements would become towns with governments and laws and regulations—none of which were much esteemed by the mountain men. The more astute among them must have realized that the two white females in the missionary party marked the end of their way of life.

The women of the party, Narcissa Whitman and Eliza Walker, did not see themselves as settlers but as those bringing the word of salvation to the "heathen savage." They viewed themselves as bound to a distant foreign land, as exotic a destination as that of their counterparts enroute to Africa or the Sandwich Islands. The real meaning of their venture was to remain hidden from them. In Narcissa Whitman's case this inability to understand and face reality was to contribute greatly to the tragedy that lay ahead for her.

She was quintessentially the 19th century "gently reared" white woman. Although encumbered with some of the more constricting views of the age, at the same time she harbored an independence of spirit and resoluteness that might in a later time have made her a suffragist or abolitionist. Whatever she might have been in a later age, she was most certainly unsuited to be a missionary to the Indians. How she came to this place in 1836 tells a great deal about the culture of the time as it applied to women like her.

Narcissa was born in 1808 in New York State, living first in Prattsburg and then in the town of Amity where her family moved when she was a young woman. Her father, Judge Stephen Prentiss, was well-to-do by small town standards and the Prentisses were pillars of the Presbyterian Church, their family and social life entirely church-centered. In a day of limited communications and cultural isolation, Narcissa's entire existence turned upon the church. She sang in the choir, read religious tomes and seemed to focus her whole intellectual and emotional life upon religion. These were the years of the Great Awakening, the spiritual revival in Protestantism that spawned an emotional evangelism of intense energy. Like many young people, Narcissa "wrestled with her soul" and achieved "conversion."

She was a bright woman, and she seems to have been the pet of her parents in a family of nine. She was also, through her blonde good looks, lively spirit and beautiful singing voice, something of a star in the small town firmament of Amity. But the choices of the time for a woman of energy, intelligence and education were indeed few; for Narcissa there was only one. When she was sixteen years old she decided to be a missionary.

Twelve years later when she actually made application to the American Missionary Board she would recall the moment of decision clearly.

> I frequently desired to go to the heathen but only half-heartedly and it was not until the first Monday of January 1824 that I felt to consecrate myself without reserve to the Missionary work awaiting the leading of Providence concerning me.

It has been suggested by Narcissa's most perceptive biographer that she was brought to this decision by the great religious wave and romanticism of the period concerning Indians and missionary work. But another reason for her yearning cannot be overlooked. For a woman of verve and talent as well as woefully limited choices, how appealing it must have been to dream of the adventure of a journey to a new land. How dramatic to cast oneself in the role of savior of the unenlightened savage.

There was in Narcissa a streak of individualism that made her out of step with the early 19th century concept of women. Yet at the same time she shared many of the concepts of her time, particularly the superiority of the educated white. These two factors guided her into her fateful decision and taken together virtually insured that her chosen goal would end in disaster.

As limited as her choices were, even that of missionary seemed to be closed to her for a while. When her application for missionary work was received by the American Board it was set aside. They would not send an unmarried woman into the field.

Shortly thereafter Marcus Whitman, a young doctor who had always wanted to be a minister, won the approval of the Board for work in the Oregon Territory. Word had come East reportedly from the Territorial Governor (no other than William Clark), of the desire of the Nez Perce Indians for the white man's God and the white man's "Book." Actually what had prompted the Nez Perce to.make the long and dangerous journey to St. Louis was not desire for the Christian religion but for the white people's "magic" which they attributed to the whites' religion. It was the power of guns and gunpowder, not Bibles and salvation, that truly interested the Indians. To the missionary-minded, however, this was a missionary call not to be ignored.

While both Whitman's and Narcissa's applications were still before the board, Whitman had come to Amity and an "arrangement" regarding his marriage to Narcissa was made. It is not known whether Whitman specifically came with the idea of securing a helpmate or whether the idea of marriage developed upon his meeting Narcissa. (At twenty-eight, though very attractive, she would have been considered an old maid—Whitman at age thirty-two was, however, a very practical man.) In any event, they decided to marry and Narcissa thereby qualified for the career she had chosen. It was a business-like arrangement typical of 19th century America.

Then Whitman decided to make the trip to Oregon on a trial basis without Narcissa. Apparently she strongly urged otherwise, but Whitman, always a very stubborn man, held to his view of the fragility of women. Both marriage and Narcissa's missionary work would have to await his return and his decision as to whether it was feasible for Narcissa to make a journey that no white woman had made before.

As it turned out he did not explore the whole route but went only as far as the site of the fur trade rendezvous, traveling with the annual caravan of trader's goods. Whitman then decided to head for home and while on the trail began preparations for bringing Narcissa out. He was now amply satisfied that she could make the journey and wrote to her from Council Bluffs:

> "I was exceedingly surprised that you should have conceived it practicable for you to have crossed the mountains this spring. Had I known half as much of the trip as I do now, when I left you, I should have been entirely willing, if not anxious, that you should have accompanied us."

Even though the marriage was an "arrangement," his decision to turn back in mid-journey and head for home, indicates that he felt a desire to be with her.

Upon his return to New York State Marcus found that in the view of the American Board it would be necessary to find more people to accompany him and Narcissa to Oregon in order to constitute a mission. Frantically Whitman hunted about for more recruits. The final choice was the most unlikely and perhaps the most unfortunate possible. The man chosen was Henry Spalding, a rejected suitor of Narcissa. Although Spalding had since married and his wife Eliza would accompany him, he still harbored bitterness at the rejection. He hated Narcissa, deemed her a fool, and kept these feeling as long as she lived.

Spalding was otherwise unsuitable as a companion for the enterprise. In addition to a very touchy ego, he was not good under stress and was prone to pettiness and bickering. His wife Eliza was of better character, a plain woman whose loveliness was internal. But she too offered problems. Only recently she had given birth to a stillborn child and was still ailing. Like many women who were to come after her on the trail, she nevertheless deemed her husband's decision to go West a command not only from her earthly master but thereby from God himself.

The Spaldings did not attend the Whitman wedding but it was an odd enough affair even without the presence of the rejected suitor. As always, church matters came first, and Narcissa's wedding was hardly more than an adjunct to the ceremony by which Judge Prentiss was made an alderman. In almost prescient fashion, Narcissa was married in a black dress. The services concluded with a hymn, Narcissa singing the last verse alone in her beautiful voice.

> Yes, my native land! I love thee;
>   All thy scenes I love them well;
> Friends, connections, happy country,
>   Can I bid you all farewell?
> Can I leave you,
>   Far in heathen lands to dwell?

The honeymoon too was odd by today's customs. Bride and bridegroom literally moved with a crowd of people. In addition to the Spaldings, they traveled with two young Nez Perce Indian boys whom Marcus had brought back from the West with him. Crossing into Pennsylvania they picked up others—the Satterlees, headed for Indian mission work just across the Mississippi, and a young woman also going there to marry her missionary fiance.

In spite of the circumstances, Narcissa fell deeply in love with her husband during the honeymoon. Like many other arrangements of the period this marriage developed into a deep bond in the face of common hard experiences. In favor of developing such a bond was the common purpose they shared and the clear and complete dependency that marriage roles of that time dictated. Further, they had brought no romantic views of love to their union and in the absence of such expectations, they had room for pleasant surprise. It was not, however, an idyllic union. Each was a strong, stubborn person and each had different values. In the years ahead this conflict would take its toll.

While still east of the Mississippi, though the journey was relatively easy through the recently settled frontier along the Ohio River, young Mrs. Satterlee, who like Eliza Spalding had obediently followed her husband despite ill health, died of what was probably tuberculosis. At St. Louis, the party received official permission of the federal government for settlement in the Nez Perce and Flathead Indian Country. The document was obliquely worded because the situation of ownership of the Oregon Territory was in doubt. The question of British vs. American claims had yet to be settled.

In St. Louis, Narcissa and the others had the opportunity to view the French city that was already the grand old lady of the frontier before Narcissa was born. Here a characteristic of the Protestant missionaries became clear. In writing to her family of a visit to the new Catholic cathedral, Narcissa gave voice to the hatred that then divided Catholic and Protestant and made some missionaries feel they were in a race to save the heathen savage.

The journey overland from St. Louis to the Rockies was probably the happiest time in Narcissa's life. In contrast, Eliza Spalding suffered grievously. The jolting ride, the scant diet, the anxiety of the journey wore on her. There was as yet no actual Oregon Trail and for a good part of the journey on the plains the missionary party was hurrying to overtake the fur company's trade caravan somewhere ahead of them. The crossing of the swollen Platte River was particularly difficult. Spalding had been injured some days earlier and the brunt of the work of swimming the draft animals across the river fell to Marcus Whitman—often in the years ahead such would be the case. For three days he labored in the swirling water until the crossing was accomplished.

In this stretch of the journey they added to their party: William Gray, an egocentric young man who, like Spalding, would make a lot of petty trouble; a hired man to drive the wagons named Dulin; another Nez Perce youth; and a young man named Miles Goodyear, who was now a greenhorn but in these twilight years of the mountain men would make a name for himself. Yet another person was now added to the venture, for here on the prairie Narcissa became pregnant.

On May 24, 1836, they finally overtook the fur company caravan. Now at least their fears concerning Indian attacks were eased. The fur train was headed by Broken-Hand Fitzpatrick, a legend even in his day; and among the rough frontiersmen were two English officers. Narcissa promptly invited the Englishmen and Fitzpatrick to tea. This scandalized Spalding and Gray, who hated Englishmen and thought Narcissa unseemly and forward. But it assuaged some of Fitzpatrick's sullenness as being encumbered with a party of greenhorns and women.

The land they crossed was virtually as unspoiled and pristine as when seen thirty years earlier by Lewis and Clark. The fur traders had left virtually no mark on the land even along the caravan route. Not until a few years later when the prairie schooners passed this way by the thousands would streams, trees, grass and game be decimated along the line of travel.

Once the Green River rendezvous was reached somehow for Narcissa the thrill of the adventure ebbed away. She fully realized how far she was going into the wilderness and how unlikely it was she would ever see her home or family again. But what seems to have disturbed her most was the nature of her encounter with the Indians. She found to her dismay that she could not relate to them. Eliza could, but Narcissa couldn't. There may have echoed in her mind something of the words of the head of the missionary board at the outset when he cautioned the Whitmans that the task before them would take profound humility. Though Narcissa had many strong points, humility was not among them.

The missionaries left the rendezvous to travel with a party of fur traders returning to Hudson Bay. At Fort Hall the party lost one of its number. Thoroughly fed up with the terrible struggle to bring along the Whitman's wagon where no other wagon had gone, Miles Goodyear turned south at Fort Hall for Utah where he became the first white man to settle in that area. One other tried to drop out; William Gray, ill from the poor diet, begged to be left by the side of the road to die. Whitman viewed this as senseless melodrama and hauled him astride a horse and the party pressed on.

The country of the Snake River was some of the worst they encountered in the long journey. Cutting through steep canyons hundreds of feet deep, the river itself was frequently inaccessible. High above its rushing water, the party looked down upon it and thirsted. "Truly I thought the Heavens over us were brass and the earth iron under our feet," Narcissa wrote in her journal.

Stubbornly, under the blazing August sun of the high desert, Whitman struggled to bring the cart on to Oregon, believing that its utility as farm vehicle outweighed the trouble. Like countless pioneers to follow, the party began to lighten their load. Spalding's books, Narcissa's little trunk of clothes, the wagon box itself and eventually the entire wagon were abandoned.

They made Fort Snake, the forerunner of Boise, a rough outpost of the Hudson Bay Company. There the party rested in deference to the women's desire to do some laundry, only their second opportunity since leaving the Missouri frontier. What followed was the most difficult kind of travel. Repeatedly they had to cross the Snake, which earns its name in part from its twisting course, but they were in the final stage of the long, long trek.

Then on August 26, the party divided at a place called Division Creek. None of the journals tells of a final dispute between the Spaldings and the Whitmans but many quarrels and reconciliations had preceded this day. It was decided that the Whitmans and the Nez Perce boys and Gray would continue with the Hudson Bay party, while the Spaldings would follow along with the cattle under guidance of an Indian called Rottenbelly.

As ominous as was this division Narcissa was now to become the first white woman to reach the Columbia River overland and would not share in history this honor with Eliza. They had come nearly four thousand miles overland, riding much of the way sidesaddle. There yet remained the treacherous descent of the Blue Mountains, but from its crest Narcissa beheld far below the thin silver trace of the Columbia and took heart.

On September 1 they reached Fort Walla Walla, a fur trade post since 1818. The worst of the journey was done and the Columbia River would hereafter be their road. They were rejoined here shortly by the Spaldings, Eliza now in good health.

The voyage down the Columbia was relatively unremarkable to the missionaries, probably now too jaded with travel to appreciate the then untrammeled grandeur of the mighty river with its rapids and abundant salmon and waterfowl. All their expectations were focused on Fort Vancouver, the British fort that was the only town in all the great Pacific West.

It should have been obvious to them at Fort Vancouver that their preconceptions of the Oregon Territory were wrong. The Whitmans and Spaldings had not come to a wilderness to serve Indians cut off totally from civilization. All around the fort were farms—established by British men who had retired from the fur trade and settled down with Indian wives. More significantly, an American missionary named Jason Lee, sent out by a rival missionary board, was already on the scene and eager for settlement by American emigrants. The Whitmans and Spaldings had arrived at that moment in which the Oregon Territory was about to become the newest frontier for American settlers.

Stubbornly however, they stuck to their original dream. As though to force it into reality the group pulled back from Fort Vancouver eastward into a wilder area. The Spaldings went alone to serve the Nez Perce tribe and the Whitmans settled on the Walla Walla River at a place called Waiilatpu.

It was foolhardy to separate again. None of them were experienced in making a home on the frontier. Further, they were dividing their strength without much prior knowledge of what relations with the Indians would actually be. In the case of the Spaldings at least the Nez Perce had demonstrated eagerness to have them in their midst. But the Whitmans' case was quite different—Marcus, for reasons unknown, chose to settle among the Cayuse tribe.

He could hardly have made a worse choice. The debilitating effect of white intrusion on the Columbia River had worked its way as far upstream as the Cayuse. The Indians there were already infected by the cultural and physical decline that generally followed the intrusion of whites' material goods, diseases, and alcohol. Even the Nez Perce warned Whitman against settling among the Cayuse, pointing out to him that the tribe was restless, discontented and rapidly depleting in numbers. But Whitman looked over the land of the Cayuse and found it good for farming. He was caught between the most effective way to serve as a missionary and the most effective way to establish a missionary outpost.

The years that followed for the Whitmans were a long, heart-breaking struggle to transplant the amenities, standards and mores of Amity, New York to the shore of the Walla Walla River. Narcissa never relinquished her narrow system of values; Marcus never thought of returning East. They persisted in the face of the hardest kind of labor, aided only sporadically by men passing through who would hire on temporarily at the tiny settlement. The Nez Perce boys who had traveled with the Whitmans grew discontented and left; William Gray decided he wanted his own property and walked out on them.

The missionary work necessarily fell back into second place. Their energies were almost completely taken up with building a house, establishing a farm, and doctoring the Indians. More often than not Marcus worked beyond the point of exhaustion, a pathetic but gallant figure taking upon his shoulders work and care enough for six men.

Narcissa, pregnant and struggling to relate to the Cayuse, worried about their very survival. When the baby came that first spring, there was no one to help with the birth except Marcus. The Indian woman who had been hired to aid Narcissa came down ill and Marcus had to care for her and her children as well as Narcissa and the new infant. Over the years the house on the Walla Walla was more an infirmary and hostel than a home. It was an inhuman burden for two people unschooled in frontier skills and grappling with unknown languages. Psychologically, it was particularly hard on Narcissa, for she still clung to the style of life now a continent away with its amenities and orderliness.

But survive they did. Marcus built the house and a barn. Fencing went up and crops were planted and harvested. Towards the end of their venture on the Walla Walla a mill was under construction. He even found time to impart to the Cayuse some agricultural skills.

Narcissa too learned how to manage—cooking, cleaning and doing laundry for hordes of people. As the Oregon Trail developed into an emigrant roadway, the annual wagon trains found help and food at the Whitman mission. Each year Narcissa met the needs of the exhausted half-starved people. On one occasion a wagon train arrived with the seven Sager children who had been newly orphaned on the trail. Narcissa took them in and became their mother.

Narcissa tried, though unsuccessfully, to be a teacher to the Indians but they remained to her an alien and inferior people. Gradually her school became almost entirely a school for white children or the children of white fathers and Indian mothers.

But she labored on, constantly re-examining her heart and her conscience as her copious letters and diaries show. She truly longed to serve God and the Indians. She was a victim of her time, thrust into an unsuitable and demanding role by her deep desire to make something significant of her life when there was no suitable channel for her talents.

In a short while the light-heartedness and bouyant energy had ebbed from Narcissa; hard work and anxiety took a heavy toll. She made her own road even harder for she still yearned for the style of life now a continent away—a genteel life with time to read, with privacy, with opportunity for prayer and thought. Especially both she and Marcus yearned for rest.

On a Sunday afternoon in their third year on the Walla Walla Narcissa paid a terrible price for a few hours of such well-earned rest. While she and her husband sat enjoying rare leisure, engrossed in their books, their own little daughter wandered from the house and drowned in the nearby river. For Narcissa, what light there had been in her hard world passed out of it. Thereafter, each time she stepped out of her door she saw the tiny grave surrounded by its white picket fence.

Her loss did not, however, embitter her. Although she was inept as a missionary and had a narrow concept of God and religion, she was a truly faithful believer. She accepted the tragedy. Her love for the only child she would ever bear, reached out to other children—among them the orphans of the Oregon Trail.

By the time the seven Sager orphans were established in the house by the river. the situation at the mission was very bad. In spite of all the visible fruits of their labors—the farm, the spacious house, quarters for travelers, a blacksmith shop—the Whitmans and the Spaldings had never been able to resolve their original conflicts. Worse, the constant flow of settlers' wagons that began in 1842 into the Oregon Territory was alarming the Indians. They had heard what had happened to their Eastern brethren when white people came to settle and now they feared they too would soon be displaced from their land. The Oregon Territory was no longer a wild Indian country but the immediate object of the American nation reaching out to extend its borders.

Then the missionaries received a terrible blow. The American Board, disturbed by the quarreling and realizing that the idea of an Indian mission had become obsolete, ordered most of the mission facilities closed and told their builders that they must come home.

Whitman looked around him at the results of his long years of hard work and decided he could not let go. It would have been a kindness to Narcissa had he done so, but he instead decided to return East and fight the Board's decision.

Even though it was winter, Marcus Whitman undertook to travel overland in what was to be a truly heroic-journey. Legend later would say that Marcus braved the terrible crossing to persuade the government in Washington to annex Oregon but that was not his real motive. He did not see the broader territorial stakes; he went to fight for his own territory—Waiilatpu and the life he and Narcissa had invested there.

In Whitman's absence, Narcissa stayed alone at the mission with only the children as companions. On a dark night she was awakened by the sound of an Indian trying to force entry into the house. Her terrified screams as she fought to hold the door caused the intruder to flee. The incident forced her to realize that she could not stay alone at the mission but before she left she had the courage to confront the chief of the Cayuse about the intruder. An Englishman at Fort Walla Walla sent a wagon for her and, in a state of depression and anxiety, she left the mission.

It had been an ominous incident but what happened next made things worse than they might have been. A self-important man named Dr. Elijah White had secured appointment as emissary of the United States government with respect to Indian relations in the Oregon Territory. In response to the attack on Narcissa he headed inland from the Willamette Valley with six armed men, determined to make the Indians submit to his white man's laws. White's show of force and his edicts, among them an *Article Nine* forbidding the keeping of dogs, predictably inflamed the Indians. Word circulated among them that Whitman had gone East to obtain soldiers for war against the Cayuse.

In his actual mission to Washington Marcus was successful. As he returned home in 1843 a new vision exploded on him. He joined a train of white-topped emigrants' wagons heading to Oregon with an unbelievable thousand new settlers. He was so dazzled by what was now happening—the surge of settlers toward Oregon—that on his return to the Walla Walla he failed to see that Narcissa was too sick and worn to continue at the mission. In his excitement over the now full-blown emigration he could not perceive her real needs for rest and to return home. Apparently, however, she tried to be brave and made no such request, at least none that is found in the records.

He also failed to see that the situation with the Cayuse Indians was now potentially dangerous. Heedless of their attitudes he turned all his attention to helping build a new land for the white settlers. The Indians watched the improvements being made in which they would have no share, and they watched Narcissa caring for her foundlings, none of them Cayuse children.

So burdened was Narcissa with children during this period that she had no time at all for even token attention to the Indians. All attempts at schooling the Cayuse had been totally abandoned. As for the missionary work, few conversions had occurred since 1836. According to the tenets of their faith, the Whitmans had to be assured of "conversion of the heart" before they would admit a new member to the church. As a consequence, in almost a decade of work among hundreds of Indians, at the Whitman mission no Indians at all had been judged qualified. Instead the Cayuse watched as the Whitmans' religion was extended to immigrant Hawaiians and to a retired white trapper.

To these resentments were added others. The Indians had never been paid for the mission lands. Instead the mission fields and gardens were fenced against the Indian horses; and Gray, before he left the Whitmans,' had poisoned some melons to sicken those Indians who helped themselves.

By 1846 hostilities were growing strong. But Marcus Whitman refused to see what might come. Apparently he counted on immigration to bring numbers enough to outbalance the Indian threat. His hopes must certainly have taken a great leap forward when in the autumn of 1846 the boundary between English and American claims was finally settled. The outposts in Oregon were now officially beneath the American flag and the Indians now anticipated the arrival of American soldiers.

Then came the final blow. The migration of 1847 brought over seven thousand emigrants to Oregon and with them came the scourge of measles. In November the disease struck the Whitman household, at this time numbering seventy-four people. Two children died almost immediately and several others were gravely ill.

Outside the mission the effects of the disease were hideous. Almost overnight the Cayuse were reduced to half their numbers. Daily the sick Indians carried their dead out from the pestilential tents where the measles victims lay ill in the midst of filth, too few of the tribe being well enough to nurse them.

The Indians blamed the whites for the terrible catastrophe that had come upon them. Whitman tried to doctor them but could do little. The time had passed when the Cayuse had any confidence in him and now he was held liable for the wave of death just as were tribal medicine men under similar circumstances. By ancient law the medicine man who could not heal had to pay with his own life.

The end came on November 29, 1847. A child of the chief had died, the third to do so. Within hours of the burial, the Cayuse attacked the mission. They first tomahawked and shot Marcus Whitman. Along with the brave, kindly doctor there died in this first attack young John Sager, one of the orphans of the trail.

The Indians then moved outside and killed four adult men who had been about their chores. In the commotion two men escaped and an emigrant family hid beneath a floor. One of the grown Sager children herded a number of the younger children into an attic over the schoolroom. In their sick beds the adults and children lay, too ill to be aware of what was happening.

In the house, Narcissa stayed calm. She dragged the dying Marcus in from the yard where he had fallen and ordered all the doors locked. But the glass panes in one door of which she had been so proud proved her destruction. Sighting from the top of a haystack, an Indian took aim and fired through the glass as she turned to look at her husband. She fell to the floor wounded. One of the orphans she had mothered tried to lift her to her feet and as the child held Narcissa, the wounded woman prayed over and over again, "Lord, save these little ones."

The children remarkably were spared as were all the other women but the Cayuse came for Narcissa, carried her outside, and killed her.

Before the massacre was done, ten men besides Whitman were dead. After a few days a rescue party arrived and the mission was evacuated. As the survivors were transported by boat down the Walla Walla River, the Indians set fire to the home so laboriously constructed.

It was a tragic ending not only for the lives cut short and the children now to be scattered and homeless, but it was also the ending of peace between whites and Indians all through the Oregon Country. A familiar cycle of reprisals, raids, and punishment set in that would continue for a decade.

In the years that followed Narcissa became a martyred figure in the legends of Oregon. The tragedy at Waiilatpu became the rallying cry for Oregon being granted full status as a state. Although it did not become a state for two more years, chiefly because of the question of slavery in the Western states, the impetus for Oregon's statehood was greatly advanced by the deaths at Waiilatpu.

Narcissa sought to sacrifice the energies of her life in missionary work but found it harder than she ever dreamed. With the perspective of time and better understanding of the rights and nature of the Indians it may seem that the whole venture at Waiilatpu was founded on error. Still she is a gallant figure, brave and persistent, the first white woman to make the long crossing to a life where she suffered much. No better monument could exist to her memory than Whitman College that stands upon the site of her mission house. It symbolizes her love of learning and once-bright dream of bringing education to the Indians.

3

Juliet Brier

Across the Desert in '49

> Every step I take will be toward California
> *Juliet Brier*

Perhaps no figure in the history of the West other than the cowboy has occupied such an important place in American folklore as the pioneer woman trudging westward alongside the white-topped prairie schooner, bound for California and brave beyond belief in the face of all manner of hardship and danger. So formidable is this figure that it is hard to believe she really existed.

Yet for once popular mythology does not outpace the truth. The story of the great Western trails is the story of heroines. There was Nancy Kelsey in 1841 with the first overland party of emigrants to California, walking 500 miles after the wagons were abandoned and carrying with her a young child. There was Mary Bulgar Murphy in 1844 with the first party to bring wagons across the Sierras, giving birth to a baby on the western slope of the last mountain range. There was Tamsen Donner in 1846, snowbound and starving in the High Sierra but refusing to leave her dying husband. And Peggy Breen, a feisty Irishwoman of this same tragic group, managed to bring her whole family through the ordeal in which half of the eighty-four emigrants died.

There is no way to tell of them all—the women who buried husband or child along the way but kept going, or those who gave birth one day on the trail and then moved on westward the next. Some indeed were broken by the hard journey and died along the way; some few turned back. But the great majority kept going and the heroic place they have been accorded in history is richly deserved.

At Salt Lake the travelers soon learned that if you were late crossing the Sierra Nevada Mountains into California you risked being trapped by violent blizzards. Like a terrible shadow, the story of the Donner Party of 1846 with its deaths and cannibalism haunted the California Trail in '49. By July, when the '49ers were coming in large numbers, the season for overland travel was growing late—the most advanced of the migration were already arriving in California. Ahead of those at Salt Lake lay another seven hundred miles of travel across the worst desert and highest mountains. Further, the earlier group could be counted on to have denuded the sparse grass of the arid lands ahead.

Thus the emigrants were faced with a cruel quandary—to go on and take grave risks in the Sierras or to stay over in Salt Lake until the next spring with food supplies almost exhausted and the good will of the Mormons uncertain. The problem was demoralizing and a fair number of emigrants remained stymied at Salt Lake, unable to resolve their dilemma.

This the Mormons would not tolerate. An eminently practical people, they realized that their fledgling settlement could not support the huge number of "gentiles" through the winter. If food supplies were short in the course of the coming of winter, the Mormons surmised that the '49ers would react with violence. (The Mormons had certainly had experience with gentile violence before escaping to Salt Lake.)

So the Mormons came up with a solution for the stalled '49ers. For a fee of ten dollars per wagon, the Mormons offered to provide a guide to lead the emigrants over an alternate route to California, one that led south to the Los Angeles area and thus avoided the danger of entrapment in the snows of the Sierras. This route involved a sizeable detour for the goldseekers since they would enter California hundreds of miles from the gold diggings, but a large number of the people like the Briers were eager to be on the move again and found the plan appealing. Perhaps some of its appeal was attributable to the fact that no less than Brigham Young himself, leader of the Mormons and a persuasive speaker, expounded the merits of the proposal in a large meeting with the emigrants.

Later many of these '49ers were to say that the proposal was no more than a Mormon trick to lure hated gentiles to their death in the desert. Others among them would assert that the Mormons exploited the '49ers in opening a new wagon road to Southern California where the Mormons planned to establish a colony. There was some truth in the second assertion. The man who was to serve as guide, Captain Jefferson Hunt, did indeed intend to establish a Mormon colony in the

San Bernardino area east of Los Angeles, and the wagon road was highly desirable from his point of view.

But there was no truth to the '49ers claim that the Mormons sent them out into the desert to die. On the contrary the Mormon leaders sent some of their own people along with Hunt, including several missionaries bound for Hawaii.

The Briers, along with the other stalled '49ers, spent the summer months encamped in a meadow area south of Salt Lake, resting and fattening their cattle while they waited for the desert weather to cool.

With the coming of October the wagon train was ready to start. Approximately one hundred wagons and four hundred people had organized themselves into what was called "The *Sand Walking* Company," a Yankee rendition of the California place-name *San Joaquin* and a title that was to prove sadly prophetic.

The route they proposed to follow was called the Old Spanish Trail though it could hardly be considered a trail at this stage in its history, nor was it necessarily Spanish. In actuality it was the western half of a route that curved from Santa Fe to Salt Lake and then southwest to the tiny settlement of Los Angeles. The eastern half of the trail was fairly distinguishable, but the western half, the part the '49ers would use, was scarcely even a dim trace on the land. Hunt, however, had been over this portion of the trail when the Mormon Battalion was mustered out after the Mexican War. (After this first journey he made a second, round-trip over the trail, this time bringing a wagon from Los Angeles to Salt Lake loaded with seeds and fruit trees for the new Mormon settlement.) The route was practical for wagons but most of the '49ers who signed up with Hunt came to believe that no wagon had ever got through. Others believed they were headed out on a well-traveled road. Both misconceptions were to cause disastrous trouble when the emigrants later began to doubt Hunt.

Hunt's personality would also apparently contribute to the coming friction. The eldest of the Brier children remembered him as a cold, aloof figure:

> The Captain was taciturnity itself. If he possessed the knowledge of a guide, he seemed to be wanting in the tact of a leader. This may be the fancy of a child, for I confess that I was afraid of the silent man, and wondered if he ever loved anybody, and if he slept on horseback.

The first few weeks went well enough until Hunt either missed a waterhole or tried for a shortcut. After thirty-six hours scouting without water, he and his companions rejoined the wagon train with their tongues literally hanging out with thirst. It was not an encouraging spectacle and the majority of the '49ers, the Briers among them, concluded that the guide didn't know his business or, even worse, was deliberately leading them into danger.

Then, near the border of Utah and Nevada, a party on horseback from Salt Lake overtook the wagon train. In the possession of the leader was a map purporting to show a "shortcut" to the mines leading directly west. If the route was feasible, the '49ers could save hundreds of miles of travel.

In actuality the westerly course proposed by the pack train led straight through the worst of the Nevada-California desert. The map itself had no relationship to reality and the meadows and watering places indicated on it simply did not exist.

More sensible men, Hunt foremost among them, argued strongly against the map and the course it showed, pointing out that it was improbable that any white man, let alone wagons, had ever gone that way. But Reverend Brier got up upon a wagon and made a stirring speech on behalf of the shortcut.

When the turn-off point indicated on the map was reached, Hunt said that he had hired on to go to Los Angeles and would go that way if even one wagon still wished to do so. Seven wagons pulled out behind him, the rest turned off on the shortcut.

Feelings were running so strongly that some of the emigrants blew up a tree to celebrate the separation from Hunt. Almost every diarist among the company remembered Hunt's words as The Sand Walking Company divided. He wished those leaving him a good journey but told them he believed they were headed "straight into the jaws of Hell."

For three days the wagons followed the pack train due west and then a gorge was reached and no way could be found to get the wagons down. The pack train easily descended the steep canyon, the leader saying he'd eat mule meat before he'd choose to turn back.

Some of the wagon people went out to search a way and in their absence a man named Rynerson mounted a wagon to make a speech.

> My family is near and dear to me. I can see by the growth of the timber that we are in a very elevated place. This is now the seventh of November, it being the fourth at the time of our turning off this trail. We are evidently in a country where snow is liable to fall at any time in the winter season, and if we were to remain here and be caught in a severe storm we should all probably perish. I, for one, feel in duty bound to seek a safer way than this. I shall hitch up my oxen and return at once to

the old trail. Boys (to his teamsters) get the cattle and we'll return.

In response to Rynerson's practical assessment, the majority of the '49ers turned their wagons one by one back toward Hunt's trail. As they rattled off to retrace their way, some of the wagons held back waiting for their scouts to come in.

Then suddenly someone shouted out that a way down the gorge had been found and with this news approximately thirty wagons were re-committed to the westward course.

Among those who now groped down the gorge were the Briers and their two hired men, Patrick and Loomis St. John. Besides Juliet Brier there were only three other women. The largest contingent was a group of men called the Jayhawkers, all of them single men or married men who had left their families at home. This tight-knit group consisted of some two dozen men who had left the same area of Illinois together and traveled the whole way as a unit bound by genuine ties of friendship.

As the '49ers struggled out of the canyon and into what was later the state of Nevada, the Briers attached themselves to a group known to historians as the "Mississippians" and to their contemporaries as the "Bugsmashers." Actually some of these men were from Georgia; one black man among them was undoubtedly a slave. One of their members, Jim Martin, was chosen captain of the party.

At this point the Bugsmashers and Jayhawkers tried to exclude the family people. The Arcanes, Bennetts and Wades accepted this decision, but Reverend Brier, as one of the party noted, "would not stay put out, but forced himself in, and said he was going with the rest, and so he did."

In the weeks that followed as they struggled across the desert, the new organization fell apart. There was only one thing that all could agree on: that it was too late to turn back and try to recover Hunt's trail. Food was almost gone and the oxen were worn out. The realization slowly came to them that they were lost. (This was probably the only major party to get into such a predicament in '49, a dubious distinction.)

The best hope seemed to be to press on due westward. At some point in the trek across Nevada, the Briers and the Bugsmashers gave up their wagons. Young John Brier ever after remembered the decision ". . . the drifting sand, the cold blast from the north, the wind beaten hill, the white tent, my lesson in the Testament, the burning of wagons as fuel, the forsaking of nearly every treasured thing, the packing of oxen, the melancholy departure.''

Relieved of their wagons, the Bugsmashers pushed ahead as rapidly as they could on foot. It was apparently a pace the Briers could not match with the children in tow and about this time they began to trail after the Jayhawkers who were still traveling slowly with wagons.

Painfully they moved across the desert, their way continually blocked by mountain ranges running north and south. There was no feed for the cattle and finding water was a constant and critical problem. In their thirst they were lured by mirages that transformed dry alkaline lakebeds into shimmering oases. Juliet Brier recalled one of these disappointments, ''Instead of water, we found it to be merely glazed mud.''

Although the parties had divided in crossing Nevada they joined together again at the point where the worst of their experience began. In the days just before Christmas the various groups dragged their way into Death Valley just west of the California-Nevada line.

But this time the Briers were straggling badly. On Christmas Eve Juliet was far behind all the others, trying to bring along both the cattle and her three little boys. Her husband was somewhere ahead—in later years she would say he always went ahead this way to look for water. Sick with thirst and weary, often falling on her knees, she kept her own little group moving all by herself.

> Poor little Kirk gave out and I carried him on my back, barely seeing where I was going, until he would say, ''Mother, I can walk now.'' Poor little fellow. He would stumble on a little way on the salty marsh and sink down, crying, ''I can't go any farther.'' Then I could carry him again, and soothe him as best I could.''

Juliet was confident that if she and the children gave out the men ahead would come back for them once they reached water but still she kept on, trying to keep sight of those ahead. It was important to her to keep going. ''I didn't want to be thought a drag or a hindrance.''

Then night came and they were all alone, unable to see those who had gone ahead or even the way to follow them. Repeatedly Juliet got down on her knees to search by starlight for tracks in the sand. ''I didn't know whether we would ever reach camp or not.'' Contrary to her expectations, no one came back for them.

At midnight on Christmas Eve she finally found her husband huddled over a little campfire. Her momentary elation was short-lived. He told her there were yet six miles to go to reach water and that night's campsite.

How Reverend Brier knew the distance yet to be traveled isn't clear. It is possible he had been to the site of the water and was now on his way back to find his family. But the campfire over which he crouched does not seem to have been set with any thought for his wife and children, for it was hidden by boulders and not visible to Juliet until she was actually upon it.

Juliet was totally spent and little Kirk was nearly unconscious for want of water. Brier rallied himself enough to carry Kirk to the springs that lay ahead. Juliet and the other two boys pushed on. It took them three hours to make the six miles.

Finally at three a.m. she stumbled into camp, wanting only to sleep. But Brier insisted she would die if she did not drink some water and eat a little from their meager supplies.

It was, she said, "a Christmas none could ever forget."

As desperate as their situation was, on Christmas Day they were better off than they had been for some days prior or would be for weeks afterward. They had reached the hot and cold springs feeding into Furnace Creek at the rim of Death Valley. The warm water provided the luxury of bathing, a luxury gratefully remembered forty and fifty years later. In commemoration of the day they slaughtered an ox to be shared freely among all present. The rest of this Christmas feast was black coffee and "a very little bread." Juliet remembered having "one small biscuit," undoubtedly of her own making.

> Nobody spoke very much, but I knew we were all thinking of home back East and all the cheer and good things there. Men would sit looking into the fire or stand gazing away silently over the mountains, and it was easy to read their thoughts. Poor fellows! Having no other women there I felt lonesome at times, but I was glad, too, that no other was there to suffer.

To help relieve the gloom, some of the men asked Brier to preach for them. The topic he chose — the value of education — seems totally inappropriate to the occasion but it probably mattered little to the dispirited men.

As the party prepared to move out across Death Valley, Dr. Fred Carr urged Juliet to stay at the springs until a relief party could be sent back. Perhaps before answering she reflected upon what had happened the previous night when no one had come back to look for her and the children. In any event her answer had in it the spirit of all of the courageous women of the trails. "I have never been a hindrance," she said. "I have never kept the company waiting, neither have my children, and every step I take will be toward California.''

In actuality they were in California but not the golden California of their dreams. Instead they were in a virtual trap. Across from their arid Death Valley camp rose the Panamint Mountains, as high as eleven thousand feet above the below-sea-level valley floor. The Jayhawkers, whom the Briers caught up with the next day, had concluded there was no way out for the wagons. When the Briers arrived the Jayhawkers were slaughtering their cattle and drying the meat in the smoke of their burning wagons.

With all of their food gone except the dried oxen meat this group realized that they were in a race with death. Everything was abandoned save one gun and the men shouldered their packs of jerked meat. While their preparations had been in progress the Bugsmashers, who had entered Death Valley by another route, came up to the campsite. They too were gripped by the necessity of speed and therefore gave the Briers their few remaining cattle before setting off to cross the Panamints.

In the exodus from Death Valley the '49ers divided into a number of groups. The Bugsmashers went one way, the Jayhawkers another and a splinter group from the Jayhawkers a third route. Further south in Death Valley yet a fourth group, containing the families and a collection of stragglers and teamsters determined to stay put at a spring they had found. They sent out two young men for help. Later this family group divided again when one man became impatient of being rescued and determined to extricate his family and his wagon by heading south. A man who tried to follow him dropped on the way and was the only person to die within Death Valley itself.

Death, however, was close to the others as they struggled to cross the steep Panamints. The mountaintops were snow-covered but the emigrants missed such springs as existed.

There was, Juliet Brier recalled,

> not a drop of water to relieve our parched lips and swollen tongues. The men climbed up to the snow and brought down all they could carry. Mr. Brier filled an old shirt and brought it to us. Some ate it while hard and relished it as though it was flowing water, but enough was melted for our frenzied cattle and camp use.

In the ordeal of crossing the Panamints, Dr. Carr again tried to persuade Juliet to turn back and he cried when she refused. ''I felt as bad as any of them, but it would never do to give up here. Give up—Ah! I know what that meant —a shallow grave in the sand.''

By this time the tiny woman was winning the respect of the Jayhawkers. She was seemingly indestructible both in spirit and body. She not only managed to bring the cattle and boys along, but saw to camp chores. "It seemed almost impossible," said one man later, "that one little woman could do so much."

If the burden of the family's survival was being carried more and more by Juliet, it was not entirely a matter of failure of Reverend Brier's character. He was, so Juliet later insisted, suffering from dysentery as well as near-starvation and was physically debilitated.

Beyond the Panamints, yet three hundred more miles remained of desert to be crossed and time was running out for them in the race for survival. On January 13, as the '49ers struggled through yet another mountain range, first one man and then a second fell and were unable to rise. No one stopped for·them. It was only when water was reached that any one had the strength to be concerned for those who had fallen. When a party went back, it was too late. Both men were dead.

All were in extremely bad physical condition, being reduced by this time to little more than skeletons. Brier had lost one hundred of his one hundred and seventy-five pounds and each morning Juliet had to help him to his feet. He was not the only one she aided; until the end of their days the Jayhawkers would remember her help and encouragement to the failing men. Since she was always at the rear trying to keep both cattle and children moving, it was she who came upon the stragglers who had fallen behind and given up. It was always she, they later insisted, who got them moving again.

Still there were those who were beyond help. A man named Robinson died in the last week of the desert crossing and an unnamed Frenchman wandered off and was assumed to have perished.

The party was now crossing the Mojave Desert, more arid even than Death Valley, and their hope was wearing thin. At nightfall beside the campfires at a dry camp, the men began to write messages of farewell to their families in the sad hope that in some way their families would thus know how they had died.

Then near the end of January, the look of the country began to change. The more sharp-eyed of the company noted signs of animals, and geese were sighted overhead. Soon they were seeing signs of horses and cattle. Then on February 1, they reached Soledad Canyon and they "were out of trouble at last."

Here were grass, streams, timber, and signs of game. A diarist of the journey wrote with joy, "It looks like home."

On February 5, they straggled in sight of an outpost of San

Francisquito Rancho. "It was," said Juliet, "like coming back from death into life again. It was a long, long weary walk, but thank God, He brought us all out of it."

Certain it is that Juliet's religious faith helped sustain her but she had a personal courage and hardihood all her own. Her own physical survival may have been in part attributable to a general female characteristic of superior biological stamina as evidenced in a number of other trail episodes in which women endured severe deprivation while men died around them. But the spirit she exhibited in keeping her family and trail companions going was beyond biology. In addition, her achievement in bringing the cattle through meant her family would have something of value with which to start life anew upon reaching Los Angeles.

The cattle she had herded were sold in Los Angeles and Brier used the proceeds to purchase a half share in a hotel. By June he was sufficiently recovered to be able to deliver the first Protestant sermon preached in Los Angeles.

No such "first" occurred for Juliet in the Brier's California life. She had made her record in the desert crossing and after arriving in California she led a quiet life, giving birth to three more children and outliving her husband and all but one son. She died just four months short of being one hundred years old.

In the course of time various of the Death Valley '49ers wrote accounts of their experience. Among those the most notable is the Western classic *Death Valley in '49* by William Lewis Manly, one of the young men who went out to get aid for the families that chose to wait in the valley. Like Juliet, Manly was a hero of the '49 episode, indeed one of the greatest in the history of the West. When he came to write of Juliet, he said, "All agreed she was the best man of the party." From a man of the time and from one like Manly, no praise could be higher.

Before anything else on the Western frontier what mattered was survival. Survive she did and with grace and courage.

4

Dame Shirley

Chronicler of Life in the Mines

I Like the wild and barbarous life
Dame Shirley

There was never a more unlikely person to come to the rough and tumble life of the California gold country in the 1850's than the woman known to history as "Dame Shirley." She was small, delicately beautiful, golden-haired and fair of skin. By her own account she had been a chronic invalid and came to the mines a "feeble and half-dying invalid." Yet this delicate Victorian lady, cultured, educated and so much a product of the hothouse Eastern culture of her time, not only survived an arduous year in the rough Sierra Nevada mountain gold camp, but immortalized the scene around her in a series of letters that have become a standard in the literature of the Western frontier and were the inspiration for several of Bret Harte's most popular short stories. No other writer among the many who tried ever approached the quality of her description of the remarkable society that sprang up in the canyons and along the rivers of the rugged Sierras, flourished for a brief season, and then suddenly passed away.

The series of letters she wrote about life in the gold camps was addressed to her sister in New England and numbered twenty-three in all, beginning on September 13, 1851, and concluding on November 21, 1852. The letters were first printed in 1854 and 1855 in a San Francisco magazine. Then for nearly seventy years they lay yellowing and generally forgotten in the scattered copies of the magazine. Not until the 1920's were they published anew.

If the priceless letters themselves languished in obscurity for a long time, the author also remained an obscure figure for an even longer period. For almost a century after she descended by mule into the deep

46

Feather River Canyon to the gold camp of Rich Bar, little was known of the life of the woman who signed herself *Dame Shirley*. Only in recent decades has the detective work of two scholars filled in the story.

Her real name was Louise Amelia Knapp Smith Clappe. She took the pen name of Dame Shirley because pseudonyms were the style on the California literary frontier, and as Dame Shirley she became one with her literary contemporaries, Mark Twain, Joaquin Miller, Old Block, and Dan de Quille.

Louise Clappe came to California with her doctor husband, Fayette, in 1849 aboard "the good ship Manilla," landing in San Francisco where the two took up residence amidst the gold madness that was turning the sleepy village of Yerba Buena into the most exciting place in the world. Springing up around her, Louise saw "flashy-looking shops and showy houses"; every luxury that money could buy was spread out for the benefit of the more fortunate gold miners. Although a far cry from her genteel and cultured New England home, San Francisco at least offered Louise a more comfortable life than she would find in the gold mines high in the Sierra Mountains a hundred miles east of San Francisco.

But the climate of San Francisco did not agree with her husband, and he was determined on moving to the gold country, reasoning that not only his health but his business might improve. He scouted out what he deemed a likely place, one of the most inaccessible gold camps and one where he judged a physician might do well.

Louise greeted the idea with spirited enthusiasm, classifying herself as "a regular Nomad," and begged him to take her with him on the initial visit. Clappe refused but subsequently wrote to her from the mountains that both could safely spend the winter there. Louise was "enchanted," although her San Francisco friends concluded "that I ought to be put into a strait jacket."

The seemingly frail little blonde had a great deal of spirit. It was present not only in her enthusiasm for the mountain adventure but seems to have been with her all her life both before and after she and Dr. Clappe set out on muleback for the hidden canyon.

At the time the two embarked on the great adventure, Louise was thirty years old and Clappe was five years her junior. For most of her life she had contended with loneliness. She had been orphaned at age seven and her six brothers and sisters were scattered among relatives. Much of her life was consequently spent traveling from home to home. To allay her loneliness she turned to books. It was a natural choice, for she came of age in the highly literary environment of Amherst. Through her associates in school and her own love of books, she became a most literary young lady, thoroughly grounded in the flowery prose style so avidly admired in that period.

Yet the fine points of literary style, the mastering of foreign languages, and the mysteries of metaphysics could not quite content her. There was apparently in her, as there was Narcissa Whitman, a longing to break out of at least the narrow geography of New England. Years before she married Clappe, Louise had expressed a longing to go to "the Far West."

In the decade between desire and fulfillment Louise attended lectures as did her circle of refined friends, taught school, and enjoyed poor health in what seems to have been the traditional fashion of the time.

Louise was involved in at least two major romances in this period and apparently several minor flirtations. One of the romances culminated in her marriage to Clappe in 1847; the other was to remain a hidden story for a hundred years.

Young Clappe was the son of a farmer turned printer and was related to Louise through her mother's family. Educated at Brown University, he had first intended to be a minister but then had switched to medicine. When the couple had been married two years he was caught up by gold fever and even though he had not yet attained his medical certification, he impetuously decided to seek his fortune in California. Undoubtedly the "regular Nomad" encouraged him and they set out around Cape Horn for the golden shore.

The young couple seemed to have engaged in outright rivalry in being invalids. Louise, who "drooped languidly" at the onset of their voyage, found herself in San Francisco, she wrote, with a husband who spent an entire year "with fever and ague, bilious remittent and intermittent fevers—this delightful list, varied by an occasional attack of jaundice." And, she noted, "the health of his purse was almost as feeble as that of his body."

From her tone it seems Louise was finding Fayette Clappe was not exactly life's perfect companion. On their rough mule trip to the mines he managed to get them lost in the middle of the night. Louise, who was rarely afraid, was on this occasion truly frightened "and besides that, was very sick with a nervous headache." After an excruciating journey and twenty-four hours in the saddle without food, Louise sobbed with fatigue. Her weariness was real enough and her fears were not too exaggerated, for she later learned that a Frenchman and his wife had been murdered near the same spot a few weeks earlier.

After a heart-stopping descent into the precipitous canyon of the Feather River, the couple were settled there in fair comfort. As the life of the mining camp caught up more and more of Louise's interests, Clappe seems to have faded considerably from her consciousness. Indeed, he seldom appears in the letters to her sister other than those times in which Louise bent to his wishes as "a dutiful wife." From what lay ahead for the couple, one can surmise that the spirited Louise found all through this period considerable strain in the marriage.

But, for the time being, life along the Feather River was all-absorbing. Something like a thousand miners clustered in the little canyon strung along the Feather. At first the Clappes settled in Rich Bar, a collection of huts of logs and canvas or pine boughs and calico. The only substantial building in sight was the "Empire Hotel." Louise described it thus:

> You first enter a large apartment, level with the street, part of which is fitted up as a bar-room, with that eternal crimson calico, which flushes the whole social life of the "Golden State," with its everlasting red—in the centre of a fluted mass of which, gleams a really elegant mirror, set off by a background of decanters, cigar vases and jars of brandied fruit; the whole forming a tout ensemble of dazzling splendor. A table covered with a green cloth,—upon which lies a pack of monte cards, a backgammon board, and sickening pile of "yellow kivered" literature,—with several uncomfortable looking benches, complete the furniture of this most important portion of such a place as "The Empire."

> The remainder of the room does duty as a shop; where velveteen and leather, flannel shirts and calico ditto—the latter starched to an appalling state of stiffness—lie cheek by jowl with hams, preserved meats, oysters and other groceries, in hopeless confusion.

> From the bar-room you ascend by four steps into the parlor, the floor of which is covered by a straw carpet. This room contains quite a decent looking-glass, a sofa fourteen feet long, and a foot and a half wide painfully suggestive of an aching back—of course covered with red calico, (the sofa, not the back,)—a round table with a green cloth, six cane-bottom chairs, red calico curtains, a cooking stove, a rocking chair, and a woman and a baby, of whom more anon—the latter wearing a scarlet frock, to match the sofa and curtains.

> A flight of four steps leads from the parlor to the upper story; where, on each side of a narrow entry, are four eight feet by ten bed-rooms, the floors of which are covered by straw matting. Here your eyes are again refreshed with a glittering vision of red calico curtains, gracefully

festooned above wooden windows, picturesquely lattice-like. These tiny chambers are furnished with little tables covered with oil-cloth, and bedsteads so heavy that nothing short of a giant's strength could move them. Indeed, I am convinced that they were built, piece by piece, on the spot where they now stand. The entire building is lined with purple calico, alternating with a delicate blue, and the effect is quite pretty. The floors are so very uneven, that you are always ascending a hill or descending into a valley.

As with her vivid description of this archetype of the gold camp hotels, Louise was able to render memorable reports on the details of her surroundings in a manner so precise that to a later generation she became virtually the single most important source of information on the long-disappeared civilization that roared its brief life in the California mountains.

Her sharp eye for detail gave us, for example, the best description of a miner's log cabin of the period, this one being especially notable, as she points out, because it was so far superior to the ramshackle lodgings most of the men provided themselves.

It is situated on the hill of which I have just been writing, and is owned by five or six intelligent, hard-working, sturdy young men. Of course, it has not floor, but it boasts a perfect marvel of a fireplace. They never pretend to split the wood for it, but merely fell a giant fir tree, strip it of its branches, and cut it into pieces the length of the aforesaid wonder. The cabin is lighted in a manner truly ingenious. Three feet in length of a log on one side of the room is removed and glass jars inserted in its place; the space around the necks of said jars being filled in with clay. This novel idea is really an excellent substitute for window glass . . .

But to return to my description of the cabin. It consists of one very large room, in the back part of which are stored several hundred sacks of flour, a large quantity of potatoes, sundry kegs of butter, and plenty of hams and mackerel. The furniture consists of substantial wooden stools, and in there I observed that our friends followed the fashion—no two of them being made alike.

Some stood proudly forth in the grandeur of four legs, others affected the classic grace of the ancient tripod, while a few, shrank bashfully into corners on one stubbed stump. Some round, some square, and some triangular in form; several were so high that when enthroned upon them, the ends of my toes just touched the ground, and others were so low, that on rising I carried away a large portion of the soil upon my unfortunate skirts.

Their bunks, as they call them, were arranged in two rows along one side of the cabin, each neatly covered with a dark blue or red blanket. A handsome oil cloth was spread upon the table, and the service consisted of tin plates, a pretty set of stone China cups and saucers, and some good knives and forks, which looked almost as bright as if they had just come from the cutlers.

For dinner, we had boiled beef and ham, broiled mackerel, potatoes, splendid new bread, made by one of the gentlemen of the house, coffee, milk, (Mr. B. has bought a cow, and now and then we get a wee-drop of milk,) and the most delicious Indian meal parched that I ever tasted. I have been very particular in describing this cabin, for it is the best built, and by far the best appointed one upon the river.

It was her desire, she told her sister, to someday write something that the world would not willingly let be forgotten, but until she came to the mines her attempts at writing were so suffused with the fancy literary fol-de-rol of the Victorian period that they are of little value. But, in the gold camp, writer and material met their natural match and Dame Shirley dropped most of the lacy overwriting to which she had been trained.

Not only was her eye sharp for physical detail, but she was capable of rendering portraits of the mining characters who crossed her path. They live in pages of her letters with a trueness to life and an almost Dickens-like vitality. Following is her description of a man known as "the Squire":

It had been rumored for some time, that we were about to become a law and order loving community; and when I requested an explanation, I was informed that a man had gone all the way to Hamilton the county seat, to get himself made into a Justice of the Peace . . . Last night I had the honor of an introduction to "His Honor." Imagine a middle-sized man, quite stout, with a head disproportionately large, crowned with one of those immense foreheads ecked out with a slight baldness (wonder if according to the flattering popular superstition, he has thought his hair off?) which enchant phrenologists, but which one never sees brooding above the soulful orbs of the great ones of the earth; a smooth, fat face, grey eyes and prominent chin, the tout ensemble characterized by an expression of the utmost meekness and gentleness, which expression contrasts rather funnily with a satanic goatee, and you have our good "Squire".

As it turned out the Squire was not successful in establishing himself as the source of law and order. By 1851 the character of the mining camps was changing and, with the easier "diggin's" disappearing, men began to steal, to suspect one another, to resent those of other races who competed for the apparently last glimmerings of the bright dream of gold. The deprivation of the hard life of mining and the boredom of a multitude of young men without the distractions of civilization needed only alcohol as the catalyst to set off mob violence in plenty.

Dame Shirley saw it steadily and saw it whole. The delicate lady did not flinch from recording the barbarities that swept the volatile community. Floggings, shootings, wild drunken brawls, a murder and lynching—all were set down with exactitude but not coldly. Perhaps the most incredible achievement of her writing was Dame Shirley's ability to see with a reporter's clear eye and yet convey her own very human reaction.

The first major act of mob violence—a lynching—occurred just two weeks before Christmas in 1851.

> He had exhibited during the trial, the utmost recklessness and nonchalance, had drank many times in the course of the day, and when the rope was placed about his neck, was evidently much intoxicated. All at once, however, he seemed startled into consciousness of the awful reality of his position, and requested a few moments for prayer.
>
> The execution was conducted by the jury, and was performed by throwing the cord, one end of which was attached to the neck of the prisoner across the limb of a tree standing outside of the Rich Bar grave-yard; when all, who felt disposed to engage in so revolting a task, lifted the poor wretch from the ground, in the most awkward manner possible. The whole affair, indeed, was a piece of cruel butchery, though that was not intentional, but arose from the ignorance of those who made the preparations. In truth, life was only crushed out of him, by hauling the writhing body up and down several times in succession, by the rope which was wound around a large bough of his green-leafed gallows. Almost everybody was surprised at the severity of the sentence; and many, with their hands on the cord, did not believe even then, that it would be carried into effect, but thought that at the last moment, the jury would release the prisoner and substitute a milder punishment . . .
>
> The body of the criminal was allowed to hang for some hours after the execution. It had commenced storming in the earlier part of the evening; and when those, whose business it was to inter the remains, arrived at the spot, they found them enwrapped in a soft, white shroud of feathery snow-flakes, as if pitying Nature had tried to hide from the offended face of heaven, the cruel deed which her mountain children had committed.

In this and other scenes she described, Dame Shirley remained faithful to a pledge she had made: " . . . I am bound, Molly by my

promise, to give you a *true* picture (as much as in me lies,) of mining
life . . . 'nothing extenuating nor setting down aught in malice.' ''
This pledge she was able to keep even through the terrible days of July
1852. "In the short space of twenty-four days, we have had murders,
fearful accidents, bloody deaths, a mob, whippings, a hanging, an
attempt at suicide and a fatal duel.''

She might also have added to her list the near-warfare between
"Americans" and "Spanish" that threatened to bloody the whole
community. Characteristically when this near-war of race hatred was at
flash-point, Dame Shirley wanted to stay and watch and was only
persuaded to seek the safety of a high hill when her husband argued
that her staying would create unbearable anxiety for others.

That she was able to write of the suicide's slashed throat, of the
hanged man's last writhings, of the amputee's final agonies, did not
mean that the violence of that July left her unaffected. The whippings
alone were a horror to her:

> Oh Mary! imagine my anguish when I heard the first blow fall upon
> those wretched men. I had never thought that I should be compelled to
> hear such fearful sounds, and, although I immediately buried my head
> in a shawl, nothing can efface from memory the disgust and horror of
> that moment. I had heard of such things, but heretofore had not realized,
> that in the nineteenth century, men could be beaten like dogs, much less
> that other men, not only could sentence such barbarism, but could
> actually stand by and see their own manhood degraded in such disgrace-
> ful manner.

By the end of the July of violence, Dame Shirley concluded that she
had indeed "seen the elephant" — a catch phrase of the gold rush that
meant one had experienced the California frontier in an unforgettable
way. She concluded her letter to her sister with her most negative note
in the long year: "Be thankful that you are living in the beautiful quiet
of beautiful A. (Amherst), . . . for believe me, this coarse, barbarian
life would suit you, even less than it does your sister.''

Perhaps the primary factor in Louise's ability to observe rather than
be overwhelmed by the barbarity around her was her growing pride in
herself as a strong person — a self-concept that her life in the East had
worked against. Referring to the horrors she had been describing to her
sister, she was yet able to exult, "And only think of such a shrinking,
timid, frail thing as I *used* to be 'long time ago', not only living right in
the midst of them, but almost compelled to hear if not see the whole.''

From the strength she had newly found in herself, she was also able
to set aside what would have been the cant response of the delicate lady

and instead be fair-minded towards the men who made up the un-
civilized world she was immersed in.

> Imagine a company of enterprising and excitable young men, settled
> upon a sandy level, about as large as a poor widow's potato patch,
> walled in by sky-kissing hills—absolutely compelled to remain, on
> account of the weather, which has vetoed indefinitely their Exodus-
> —with no place to ride or drive, even if they had the necessary vehicles
> and quadrupeds,—with no newspapers nor politics to interest them
> —deprived of all books but a few dog-eared novels of the poorest
> class—churches, lectures, lyceums, theaters, and (most unkindest cut of
> all!) pretty girls, having become to these unhappy men mere
> myths,—without one of the thousand ways of passing time peculiar to
> civilization,—most of them living in damp, gloomy cabins, where
> Heaven's dear light can enter only by the door,— and when you add to
> all these disagreeables the fact that, during the never-to-be-forgotten
> month, the most remorseless, persevering rain which ever set itself to
> work to drive humanity mad, has been pouring doggedly down, sweep-
> ing away bridges, lying in uncomfortable puddles about nearly all the
> habitations, wickedly insinuating itself beneath un-umbrella-protected
> shirt-collars, generously treating to a shower-bath and the rheumatism
> sleeping   bipeds,   who   did   not   happen   to   have   an   India-
> rubber-blanket—and,   to   crown   all,   rendering   mining   utterly
> impossible,—you cannot wonder that even the most moral should have
> become somewhat reckless.

Another thing which gave Dame Shirley her remarkable balance was
a resiliance of character that was composed of equal parts humor and
determination. All through her letters there is a lightheartedness that
repeatedly reasserts itself after each trying episode. She seemed bent
on taking nothing *too* seriously and on making the absolute best of
everything. She understood in some way that she was not enduring but
adventuring and in consequence was able to see her life and herself
with the journalist's dispassionate eye. So determined was she to be
courageous and cheerful that when famine threatened the snowbound
community she sought to reassure her sister that there was no real
danger. If it was a bit of whistling in the dark, it was well done. Louise
left to the world not only a remarkable record of mining life, she also
recorded the extraordinary movement of one woman from the
stereotype of feminine frailty to sturdy confidence.

She also left a perceptive record of how other women fared on the
Western mining frontier. From her writings as one of a handful of
women among a thousand men we know much about how greatly
women were valued under such circumstances. She herself was ever

the honored guest of the entire community, but it was not her blonde hair alone which won her the veneration of the miners. As she noted, any woman would be indulged to any degree and on one occasion a trial was moved so as not to inconvenience a barkeep's wife who wanted to attend.

Similarly, on an otherwise wearing trip to a political convention to which Clappe had been elected a delegate, Dame Shirley delighted in describing the character of the immigrant women she met who had newly arrived overland by covered wagon. Among them her own favorite was the *long woman*.

> But the most interesting of all my pets was a widow, whom we used to call the "long woman." When but a few weeks on the journey, she had buried her husband, who died of cholera after six hours illness. She had come on; for what else could she do? No one was willing to guide her back to her old home in the States; and when I knew her, she was living under a large tree a few rods from the rancho, and sleeping at night, with all her family, in her one covered wagon. God only knows where they all stowed themselves away . . . with "nine small children and one at the breast," . . . . People used to wonder what took me so often to her encampment, and at the interest with which I listened to what they called her "stupid talk." Certainly there was nothing poetical about the woman . . . She was immensely tall, and had a hard, weather-beaten face, surmounted by a dreadful horn comb and a heavy twist of hay-colored hair, which, before it was cut and its gloss all destroyed by the alkali, must, from its luxuriance, have been very handsome. But what interested me so much in her, was the dogged and determined way in which she had set that stern, wrinkled face of hers against poverty. She owned nothing in the world but her team, and yet she planned all sorts of successful ways, to get food for her . . . large family . . . She made me think of a long-legged, very thin hen, scratching for dear life, to feed her never-to-be-satisfied brood. Poor woman! she told me that she was compelled to allowance her young ones, and that she seldom gave them as much as they could eat, at any one meal.

Upon her return from the mountain political convention, Louise found that the end was near for the camps along the Feather River. The gold had run out and the communities that had been so seemingly vigorous began to die. On November 21, 1852, Dame Shirley wrote her last letter to sister Molly in which she told her that "to our unbounded surprise . . . nearly all the fluming companies had failed—contrary to every expectation." These fluming operations had represented the miners' laborious and expensive attempt to get to the bedrock which they believed would contain the gold no longer to be found on the surface.

"Of course the whole world, *our* world, was, to use a phrase much in vogue here, 'dead broke.' The shopkeepers, restaurants, and gambling houses, with an amiable confidingness peculiar to such people, had trusted the miners to that degree that they themselves were in the same moneyless condition. Such a batch of woeful faces was never seen before, not the least elongated of which was F's (Fayette)—to whom nearly all the companies owed large sums."

At the time of her writing the foregoing, the population of her community had shrunk to only twenty persons "although two months ago, you could count them up by the hundreds."

Louise and Fayette had scheduled their departure but when the "expressman" (actually a mule team owner) arrived at the hour appointed for leaving, Clappe was not present, having gone to visit a sick friend several days' journey away.

The mule driver refused to wait even one day for fear of being caught in a snowstorm and the Clappes' friends urged Louise to take this possibly last chance to get out of the mountains while the way was still open. "It was the general opinion from the unmistakable signs, that the rainy season would set in a month earlier than usual, and with unusual severity." But leaving without her husband was something Louise would not consider. "This I decidedly refused to do, preferring to run the fearful risk of being compelled to spend the winter in the mountains, which—as there is not enough flour to last six weeks, and we personally have not laid in a pound of provisions—is not so indifferent a matter as it may at first appear to you."

As she hung on, waiting for Clappe and facing possible entrapment in a Sierra winter, Dame Shirley recorded the scene of the dead mining town.

> . . . a large pile of gravel prevents me seeing anything else; but by dint of standing on tiptoe, I catch sight of a hundred other large piles of gravel . . . —excavations of fearful deepness, innumerable tents, calico hovels, shingle palace, ramaras, (pretty, arbor-like places, composed of green boughs, and baptised with that sweet name,) half a dozen blue and red-shirted miners, and one hatless hombre, in garments of the airiest description, reclining gracefully at the entrance of the Humboldt, in that transcendental state of intoxication, when a man is compelled to hold on to the earth for fear of falling off. The whole Bar is thickly peppered with empty bottles, oyster cans, sardine boxes, and brandied fruit jars, the harsher outlines of which are softened off by the thinnest possible coating of radiant snow. The river, freed from its wooden flume prison, rolls gradually by.

And in sad mood she looked about her at the remnants of her own life during the great adventure. What had seemed a cozy cabin looked considerably different to her from when she and Fayette had first set up housekeeping.

> I wish that you could see me about these times. I am generally found seated on a segar-box in the chimney corner, my chin in my hand, rocking backwards and forwards (weaving, you used to call it,) in a despairing way, and now and then casting a picturesquely hopeless glance about our dilapidated cabin. Such a sad looking place as it is! Not having been repaired, the rain pouring down the outside of the chimney—which is inside of the house—had liquefied the mud, which now lies in spots all over the splendid tin mantle-piece, and festoons itself in graceful arabesques along the sides thereof. The lining overhead is dreadfully stained, the rose-garlanded hangings are faded and torn, the sofa-covering displays picturesque glimpses of hay, and the poor, old worn-out carpet is not enough to make india-rubbers desirable.

Suddenly, while Louise was writing this last letter to her sister, her husband entered with the ''joyful news'' that an expressman had arrived who would take them out the next day provided they would leave behind their trunks and other possessions. Already snow was five foot deep in the higher elevations and Louise was ready to go. ''We shall leave tomorrow, whether it be rain or snow, for it would be madness to linger any longer.''

But it was hard for her to go. Perhaps she had a feeling that this had indeed been the central experience of her life. ''My heart is heavy at the thought of departing forever from this place. I *like* the wild and barbarous life; I leave it with regret . . . Yes, Molly, smile if you will upon my folly, but I go from the mountains with a deep sorrow. I look kindly to this existence, which to you seems so sordid and mean. Here, at last, I have been contented. The 'thistle-seed,' as you call me, sent abroad its roots right lovingly into the barren soil and gained an unwonted strength in what seemed to you such unfavorable surroundings.''

She had become not only physically stronger—''perfectly healthy,'' as she boasted to her sister—but had gained inner strength. ''Really, everybody ought to go to the mines, just to see how little it takes to make people comfortable in the world.''

Closing her letter late at night she bade farewell at midnight to the ''solemn fir trees,'' the mountains around her, and ''the beloved, unconventional wood-life . . . I quit your serene teachings for a restless and troubled future.''

Louise and Fayette made their way back to San Francisco only to part. She had, as one commentator has said, "shown loyal support of her improvident husband," but Fayette left her and went to the Hawaiian Islands. On April 5, 1857, a San Francisco newspaper noted that Louise Clappe had been granted a divorce.

Of her life thereafter one of the few commentators who has written of her noted, "From that day Shirley was alone; she who had loved children but had borne none, spent many years teaching in the old Denman Grammar School, mothering her niece, encouraging the more brilliant of her students to write, and delivering lectures on art and literature to members of her salon."

This portrayal of the years after Clappe deserted her may or may not be correct in its essential melancholy. Whether the loss of her husband was really important to her cannot be precisely known.

But almost a hundred years later a clue emerged as to what Louise may have really treasured in her life. A packet of letters was found in New Jersey in recent years by an historian revealing an important relationship that occurred in the decade prior to her marriage to Clappe. The circumstances sound like a Victorian novel.

These letters were not written by Louise but to her. They came regularly between 1837 and 1847, numbering forty-six in all and were written by Alexander Everett, a scholar, diplomat and in his time literary figure of considerable prominence. He had met Louise in 1837 when she boarded a coach carrying, as he always remembered, a little pot of flowers.

In the course of this coach ride Everett fell in love with the young woman half his age who engaged in eager conversation with him about books and art. It seems they never saw one another again but over the years they corresponded faithfully as Everett moved from one diplomatic post to another. He counseled her in intellectual pursuits and it was he who encouraged her to write: "If you were to add to the love of reading the habit of writing you would find a new and inexhaustible source of comfort and satisfaction opening upon you."

Over the years he grew more open in expression of his feelings for her. By 1839 he urged her to consider him her "real and sincere friend," and by 1840 she was addressed as "my fair traveling companion." By 1841 he offered himself as a lover "Platonic, of course, . . . being married and of unctuous age." But Louise apparently did not encourage him and in 1847, when he was told by her of the coming marriage to Clappe, Everett did not respond to the news good-naturedly in his letter of reply. (Later that year he died in

Macao.)

Though Louise rejected him as a lover she took his advice about writing and began even before she left New England. Everett helped her to get one item published in an Eastern periodical and after she came to California she published several "Dame Shirley" letters in a Marysville newspaper. These pieces and the ones she wrote after leaving the mines are far short of the calibre of the famed Shirley letters from the Feather River.

The quality of the letters from the mines has been attributed to the possibility that Louise never intended them for publication and therefore wrote more naturally than she would have had she followed the literary standards of the day. Yet the letters do show a considerable amount of conscious work. Further, Louise made copies of the letters which, through a Marysville newspaperman, eventually were published in the periodical, *The Pioneer*.

The Shirley letters were highly valued by several prominent contemporaries of Louise. Josiah Royce, California's first true intellectual and noted American philosopher, said they were "the best account of an early mining camp that is known to me." Charles Stoddard, one of her pupils in San Francisco and later a member of the city's literary clique, said that "the true stories she had written were to Bret Harte's fiction as champagne is ahead of soap suds."

Harte based incidents in several of his most famous short stories upon the Shirley letters and it was Stoddard's contention that Harte had suppressed Louise's work out of fear her material would outshine his own.

In 1878 Louise left San Francisco and returned East where she lived with her niece and did some writing and lecturing. In 1897 she retired to a home (which was, incidently, run by Bret Harte's nieces) in New Jersey and there she died in 1906 at the age of eighty-six.

At her death the packet of letters from Everett was found near her. Everett had set her upon the path of being a writer and the world, as well as Louise, owed him a great deal.

But for her own personal growth that year in the mine—the inner growth that made her vision and quality of writing possible—Louise owed no credit to anyone. In the wild setting of the mountains she reached into the innermost fibre of her nature and brought forth the strength and clarity of vision that produced a classic of Western literature.

Donaldina Cameron *Photograph Courtesy of Cameron House San Francisco*

Minority Women in the West

Juanita, Biddy Mason, Donaldina Cameron

Before me was sweet freedom's plains
Black Folk Song

The tiny gold rush town of Downieville, California, still clings to life high up in the Sierra Nevada Mountains. It is crammed against a towering mountainside and seems to live in perpetual shadow. It was here on July 5, 1851, that there occurred one of the most outrageous incidents on the California frontier: the lynching of a woman by a mob of miners.

The woman's name was Juanita. She was termed a "Mexican" but could actually have been any of the Latin American nationalities. Accounts of her character and of the murder of which she was accused vary considerably but the lynching itself is well-documented.

The tragedy was set in motion by a riotous, drunken Fourth of July celebration typical of the goldmining camps. During the course of the wild night a drunken miner named Cannon came to Juanita's cabin and broke down her door. Whether more occurred is not known although one tradition maintains that Cannon either raped Juanita or tried to.

The next day Cannon returned to Juanita's house—sober and apologetic, his friends later maintained. He did not appear thus to Juanita, however. Whatever passed between the two, at this point Juanita seized a knife and stabbed Cannon.

The murder was clearly unpremeditated and Juanita was likely acting out of a sense of self-defense or, as some have argued, to protect her lover Jose, who was present when Cannon returned and may have become involved in a fight with the "gringo."

But these points got little consideration from Cannon's friends. Almost instantly they gathered a mob—Cannon having been very popular in Downieville. Juanita was seized and a so-called court was convened. The miners voted to expel Jose and his "evil" friends. Juanita was sentenced to hang.

Several brave men spoke out in her defense, one of them being Stephen Field, later a justice of the State Supreme Court. A doctor present testified in support of Juanita's plea that she was pregnant. All arguments were, however, in vain. She was hanged from the town bridge by "the hungriest, craziest, wildest mob."

Though many of the facts of the case have been disputed ever since that July day in 1851, there is one factor in the lynching that seems indisputable: had Juanita been a "white" woman, she would not have been executed for the killing, even if it had been cold-blooded and premeditated. So venerated were white women on the California mining frontier because of their rarity that they were actually valued by men almost beyond life itself. The same male populace of Downieville that could lynch a non-white woman would on another occasion vote to leave the town and face the snows of the Sierras so that the dwindling food supplies would be conserved for the white women. But such gallantry was for white women only. Toward women of color the male attitude was much different, as in the case of Juanita.

This marked difference in attitude had not always dominated the Western frontier. The first Yankees who had come to California in the decades preceding the gold rush had readily married the "Californias," the women of Spanish-Mexican decent. Similarly, from the earliest white penetration of the trans-Mississippi west, the explorers, mountain men, traders and trappers had frequently married Indian women.

The coming of white women to the frontier, even in small numbers, radically changed the picture. Their very presence, though they were few and far between, somehow reduced the status of Indian or Spanish-Mexican women. Many of the men who had previously lived contentedly with Indian women, for example, were now dubbed "Squaw men" and a number abandoned their wives in the face of social stigma. As the virulent racism of the times thus asserted itself on the frontier women of color became despised objects considered fit, if for anything, only for physical abuse, sexual exploitation, or slavery.

In the psychology of the times the women of despised nationality or races were also considered to be evil. When the miners of Downieville were reproached in the press for their brutality in lynching a woman, they insisted that Juanita was a prostitute and that, in executing her, they had not only exacted punishment for a murder but for the corruption wrought among them by Juanita's influence.

Sharp-eyed and astute, Dame Shirley noted the same attitude among the miners of Rich Bar who drove from their midst a Latin-American woman.

> Some went so far as to say, she ought to be hung, for she was the *indirect* cause of the fight. You see always, it is the old, cowardly excuse of Adam in Paradise: the *woman* tempted me, and I did eat. As if the poor, frail head, once so pure and beautiful, had not sin enough of its own . . . without being made to answer for the wrong-doing of a whole community of men.

Some women fought back physically. Juanita was among them and so was the "Mejicana" of Rich Bar who, Dame Shirley said, "fought like a very fury." But a woman can seldom win a physical fight against a mob of males. Without the protection of men of her own group or the protection of the laws, she was subject in a violent era to the most terrible kinds of violence. In the California mining area Latin American men tried to protect their women but the Anglo- Americans viewed this not as gallantry but as impudence and as a justification in part for the repeated attempts to drive the Latin Americans from the mines. It is no accident of myth-making that the legendary Joaquin Murietta, famed bandit of frontier California, is portrayed in myth as having been driven to a life of crime when Anglo-American men assaulted his wife, Rosita. In the Latino version of the Joaquin saga, Rosita rides by his side in the raids of vengeance upon the Yankees.

As for the California Indians, they were unarmed for the most part and generally a gentle people and the males could do little to protect their women against the Anglos with their guns and mounted strength. The story of the treatment of the California Indians is one of the worst in America's ugly history of race relations.

Worse than the racism that victimized women of color was the sexism within racism, particularly with the denial of protection of the laws to women of color. In those instances where males of color were systematically being deprived of the protection of the law, similar deprivation toward women was perhaps not too surprising. What is particularly appalling is that women of color on the frontier continued to be deprived of basic protection of the law long after it was extended to men of their group. In California, for example, even as late as the 20th century women had to fight the inequity or inadequacy of the law itself to escape slavery or enforced prostitution.

One of the pioneers in fighting slavery of both men and women in

California was Biddy Mason, a black woman born into slavery in Hancock County, Georgia, on August 15, 1818. In 1838 she was living in Missouri where her eldest daughter, Ellen, was born. Ten years later Biddy was the mother of two more daughters, and the family of four were the slaves of a man named Robert Smith and were living in Mississippi.

In about 1848 Smith and his wife moved from Mississippi to Utah. Undoubtedly the Smiths had been converted to Mormonism, since few non-Mormons went to settle in Utah before 1849 and the Mormons were one of the very few Western communities that upheld the institution of black slavery. The Smiths took with them to Utah not only Biddy Mason and her three daughters but a woman slave named Hannah and her two sons and two daughters. The Smiths and their slaves stayed several years in Salt Lake City and then, when Smith's wife became ill, he decided to join a Mormon wagon train to California in 1851.

The Mormon caravan numbered some three hundred ox-drawn wagons. Down the long desert route from Salt Lake to Los Angeles Biddy trailed the wagons, herding the large number of loose stock. Along with her work in driving the herd of cattle, Biddy had the care of her three young children, in itself a formidable task on the trail.

Unlike Utah, the state of California had outlawed slavery in its 1850 constitution principally because the miners feared the competition of forced labor in the mines. Under terms of federal law, however, a slave owner retained ownership of his slaves even when on free soil. California attempted to resolve this conflict of law by establishing the principle that a slave owner could retain his slave property only if he were "in transit" through the state.

In point of fact, few people came as far as California with their slaves merely to visit nor were they ordinarily just passing through the state en route to somewhere else. The "in transit" principle was a mockery therefore, existing only on paper to appease those who opposed the establishment of slavery in California as a recognized institution. The "in transit" law was not enforced in any systematic way and there were, as a consequence, a fair number of black slaves in California despite the fact that California was a free state.

The black slave in a wagon train headed for California, however, rejoiced at the prospect of getting to the golden state. It was, after all, a free state and thus offered the possibility of escape to freedom. In addition the prospect of being able to pan for gold—a dream of riches for white men—was for blacks a dream of freedom. One could, hopefully, earn enough to buy freedom from the master and then buy the freedom of relations still held in slavery in the South. A black song of the time expressed the hope of the black pioneers in the wagon trains headed west:

> "Behind I left the whips and chains,
> Before me was sweet Freedom's plains."

Once Biddy and Hannah and their children arrived in California they continued as slaves to the Smiths in San Bernardino. Here Biddy's daughters—Ellen, Ann and Harriet—grew to ages fifteen, thirteen, and six respectively. There can be little doubt that Biddy must have had great anxiety for the daughters approaching womanhood. One of Hannah's daughters, fifteen-year-old Ann, gave birth to a baby girl in 1854 and undoubtedly this was Smith's child. So long as the women and girls were held slaves even in "free" states they would be subject to the same indignities suffered under systematic Southern slavery. In the midst of freedom Biddy could only look forward to her daughters having to bear yet another generation of children born into slavery.

Then, in 1854, even a more disturbing possibility arose. Smith decided to move his family and his slaves to Texas. For Biddy and the others this was the worst thing that could happen. So long as they remained in a free state the chance of getting out of slavery by some means was alive, but if they were taken back to a slave state such as Texas, freedom was in all probability lost to them forever.

Tradition credits Biddy herself with making the fight for their freedom. Actually she needed help in bringing the court case that now ensued. Under California's Right of Testimony Act no black, Indian or person of mixed blood could testify in a suit against a white person. The legal action therefore had to be brought by a white.

Through an intermediary Biddy secured the help of the sheriff of Los Angeles as Smith moved his entourage through that city before heading east. The sheriff, Frank Dewitt, sought a writ to prevent Smith taking Biddy and the others out of the state and back into a slave state on the grounds that Smith had not been in California "in transit" but had actually resided in the state and thereby had forfeited the right to keep his slaves or force them to leave the state.

On January 19, 1856, the district judge of Los Angeles ruled that "all the said persons of color are entitled to their freedom and are free and cannot be held in slavery or involuntary servitude." The "said persons" by this time included the infant son of Hannah, only two weeks old at the time of the judge's decision.

Fortunately for the former slaves, Smith did not take his case up on appeal to the State Supreme Court; the next year that court decided the Archy Lee case in a way similar to the Mason case but awarded Lee to his master on the incredible grounds that the ''in transit'' principles involved were rather new and the owner couldn't have been expected to understand them. A wag of the time commented that this was a way of ''awarding the law to the North and the slave to the South.''

Biddy's successful reach for freedom was an important contribution to her people because it showed that basic inequity of law could be overturned. All up and down the state free blacks and their white cohorts took heart from the case, encouragement they would need in the face of later decisions such as the Archy Lee case. Money was collected for more court cases to aid other blacks held as slaves.

As late as 1869, six years after the Emancipation Proclamation officially ended slavery in the United States, two young black women—Belle Grant and Hester Anderson—were found still being held in slavery in the California town of Red Bluff and were rescued. On June 3, 1872, almost a decade after the Emancipation Proclamation, a black woman named Annie Durham was aided in escaping her owner in Stockton, California. The tragedy, of course, was that the law was so long in becoming effective for these women.

Even for the blacks who secured freedom in California before the Emancipation Proclamation, life was still perilous in the 1850's and early 1860's. Without a good set of Freedom Papers and access to a quick-moving attorney, a black could be claimed as a runaway slave by any glib white. Those blacks who were secure from such threat still faced the possibility of losing property they had acquired through homesteading because of the racial bias of California's laws.

Even in the face of such inequities, Biddy Mason chose to stay in California once she gained her freedom and immediately set about becoming a financial success. For two dollars and fifty cents a week she took a job as ''confinement nurse'' for a Los Angeles doctor. From these wages she not only supported herself and three daughters but saved enough to begin buying property.

Her first acquisitions were two lots between Spring and Broadway Streets in Los Angeles. She continued acquiring property in what was then considered the outskirts of town, reasoning that growth would soon reach the area that was, in fact, to become downtown Los Angeles.

Through her foresight in acquiring property and her tenacity in hanging on to it, she was able to build up a respectable fortune. By

1919 the author of *Negro Trail-Blazers of California* compared Biddy Mason to Wall Street's Hetty Green and termed Biddy "the most remarkable pioneer of color coming to California."

From accounts such as that quoted above one can conclude Biddy's financial acumen made her a hero to the black community every bit as much as had her successful reach for freedom in 1854. As the "leading trail blazer in finance of the Negro race," she not only inspired her people but made her fortune of direct benefit to others. She gave liberally to the support of her church and aided the poor, and her home became "a refuge for stranded and needy settlers." She also gave liberally of herself, visiting the jails and hospitals and becoming known as "Grandma Mason." In her old age she was recognized by the *Los Angeles Times* in a 1909 article as "well-known" throughout Los Angeles County for her charitable work." Among her most remembered contributions to the community was her bearing of the cost of food for the refugees of a destructive flood in the 1880's.

Ellen, her eldest daughter, married two years after the Masons settled in Los Angeles. As a slave Ellen had had no education and later in life she went to school with her children, one of whom became a prominent Los Angeles businessman.

The middle daughter, Harriet, also married but little is known of her subsequent history. Ann, the youngest, died within a few years of being freed. In 1891 Biddy Mason died in Los Angeles at the age of seventy-three, one of the most famous and respected pioneer blacks in the West.

About ten years before Biddy Mason's life ended, a young woman who was the daughter of well-educated Scottish immigrants left a comfortable life on a Southern California ranch to become perhaps the most active and daring freedom fighter in the history of the West. Her name was Donaldina Cameron but in a short time after she entered her new life she became known as "Lo Mo," Chinese for "The Mother," and as such she became a terror to the slave dealers of San Francisco.

Although Donaldina's exploits began near the end of the 19th century, San Francisco was still at that time very much a frontier city, wild, garrish, full of sin and easy money. The inhuman Chinese slave trade that had begun in San Francisco's earliest gold rush days continued unabated at the time Donaldina arrived on the scene, forty-five years after the trade had first begun.

During sixteen years of this period between 1850 and 1895 a woman named Margaret Culbertson had carried on a virtual one-woman battle to free Chinese girls held in slavery. In her work she had been aided by a group of Protestant women to the extent that the group financed a home for girls who were freed. But the work of actually freeing the girls was Margaret Culbertson's. She became Donaldina's mentor until her death, soon after Donaldina joined her in slave raiding. Then Donaldina took over the job.

Donaldina had little preparation for the bizarre career she suddenly undertook. She was motivated by nothing more than the query, "Don't you want to do something?", directed at her by a respected older woman visiting on the Southern California ranch where the Cameron family was living. The impulsive Donaldina seized on the invitation to assist Margaret Culbertson and thus began a forty-year career. "I just stepped into that great task," Donaldina recalled years later, "in no way guessing what lay ahead, in no way prepared to undertake it."

A lot of learning was crammed into the eighteen months between Donaldina's arrival in San Francisco and Margaret Culbertson's death. At the refuge for freed slaves at 920 Sacramento Street in San Francisco, Donaldina barely had a chance to learn the dimensions of the slave problem and the problems associated with running the refuge where the rescued women of Chinatown were rehabilitated for a new life.

It is scarcely fair to term them women. Many of the slaves hidden in Chinatown's teeming alleys and crannies were girls as young as ten or twelve. In some cases slavers actually owned girl babies whom they would raise to a more profitable maturity as household slaves or prostitutes.

> The girl slave's life was cruel to the extreme. Of course they got neither the payment for their sale or debauching, nor any of the income from their prostitution. They went out a few times a month under heavy guard to "take the air." The rules were like those of a medieval prelate's prison. Beatings were common, and burning with a hot iron was done, but since that would mark the merchandise it was only for extreme cases. Failure to please a customer of any kind and in any condition brought starvation, flogging . . . Some people who have studied the condition have stated that a crib girl lasted from six to eight years at her degrading task. The frugal owner, when a girl became diseased, broken-minded, senile before her time, often made her "escape" to the Salvation Army, thus avoiding the problem of disposing of a worn-out item. If the owners of slave girls had to end the career of a crib inmate themselves, they provided what were called "hospitals."

Another newspaper reporter found conditions grim.

> When any of the unfortunate harlots is no longer useful and a Chinese

physician passes his opinion that her disease is incurable, she is notified that she must die . . . Led by night to this hole of a "hospital," she is forced within the door and made to lie down upon the shelf. A cup of water, another of boiled rice, and a little metal oil lamp are placed by her side . . . Those who have immediate charge of the establishment know how long the oil should last, and when the limit is reached they return to the "hospital" unbar the door and enter . . . Generally the woman is dead, either by starvation or from her own hand . . .

To be rescued from such a fate, or to escape once enslaved, was extremely difficult. Many of the girls were still helplessly young in years when kidnapped in China or purchased from poor parents. They were kept under strict guard and smuggled into the United States. A white madam wrote of the trade in her memoirs: "When I got to San Francisco in 1898, I had as a laundry woman an old harridan named Lai Chow, who was once a slave girl, brought in for the sports in Little China (Chinatown). She told me she came in with twelve-year-old girls, two dozen of them in padded crates billed as dishware."

Once in the houses of their new owners, the girls were closely guarded. They were also barred from escape from Chinatown by their ignorance of the country and its language and many were made to fear the white society by the tales told them by their owners, no stories being more lurid than those fabricated about *Fahn Quai,* the name given Donaldina by the slaves, a name meaning White Devil.

This "White Devil" was a tall, inspiring woman with coppery hair. She was born in New Zealand in 1869, the youngest of six children. Shortly after her birth her family tried ranching in New Zealand for a short period before moving to California where Donaldina's father became manager of the famous Lucky Baldwin ranch in Southern California. Although the mother of the family died when Donaldina was five years old, the family remained close knit, full of fun and devoted to their heritage of literature, religion and tales of the Scottish chiefs. It was these stories, so Donaldina recalled as an elderly woman, that gave her courage when her rescue raids involved danger.

That there would be danger she learned in the very beginning. Almost as soon as she joined Margaret Culbertson at 920 Sacramento Street, a stick of explosives was found planted in the building with sufficient power to have leveled the entire block.

Generally, however, the great challenge lay not in raw courage but in clever maneuvering. Typically word would come that a slave girl wanted to escape. If all went well, Donaldina would get the cooperation of the police, secure a warrant, and with a San Francisco police officer in tow, she would lead her little raiding party in search of the waiting girl.

The search itself took speed and astuteness, for the girls were often well hidden behind a maze of secret panels and hallways. One hunt ended when Donaldina found the girl she sought, along with another slave, hidden in a box-like enclosure between the floor and ceiling of a two-story house.

If word that the White Devil was coming preceded the raid, the slaver would try to smuggle the girl away through the dark, narrow alleys of Chinatown. Sometimes girls were hurried away over the rooftops. But Donaldina was quick in pursuit and in time developed an instinct for where the quarry might emerge and stationed a policeman or assistants from the refuge to watch the possible exit.

It took time though for her to learn the tricks of the slavers and the ways to outsmart them. In the beginning, when she was still a novice, she made the mistake of allowing a slave owner to look over the girls in the refuge in search of one whom he alleged had stolen some property before escaping. Donaldina didn't realize that the ruse of accusing a girl of theft and bringing a warrant for her arrest was a quick way of recapturing a slave. In her naivete she called the girls together, confident that none of them were thieves and that therefore none had run away from this particular man.

Warrant in hand and aided by the police, the slaver grabbed one of the girls out of the line-up and dragged her away under the false theft charge. Donaldina lost no time in pursuit and trailed them to Palo Alto, home of the newly established Stanford University. Here the slaver was abetted by the local sheriff to such extent that the university community was enraged, and the students marched in protest and actually tore off part of the local jail.

But the actual re-rescue of the girl was left to Donaldina. At one point in the pursuit she flung herself into the buggy carrying the girl away but was thrown out onto the ground by the abductors. In spite of the fact that the owner coerced the girl through a hasty wedding ceremony, Donaldina was able to convince federal authorities that the girl was in the country illegally. When next the girl was located and the matter brought to trial, the federal authorities moved in to take official custody. The attorney for the slaver made one final attempt to secure the girl by force. He spirited her from the courtroom and was about to whip up his horses when a Federal officer overtook him and grabbed the horses' reins.

Not all of the rescues involved such dramatic actions. Periodically a conscientious immigration man would become suspicious of the story of a "father" or "husband" bringing the "daughter" or "wife" into the United States. When this happened, Donaldina was alerted and procedures were set in motion to get the girl safely into the refuge. Complicating these rescues, however, was the fear under which the slavers held the girls, many of whom continued to support the bogus story of the "father" until they felt themselves truly safe within the walls of 920 Sacramento Street.

One of the earliest of the immigration episodes involved a baby girl who was being brought through immigration by an old woman alleging to be her grandmother. In actuality the old woman had purchased the baby in Hong Kong for ten dollars. When the ruse was exposed the young superintendent of the immigration facilities wanted to keep the baby in San Francisco where its welfare could be insured. He was, however, ordered by his superiors in Washington to deport the baby on the next China-bound ship.

When Donaldina learned that the infant was to be sent back to China where undoubtedly she would be resold, she coolly picked it up and walked off with it. Through her special pleading with an official in the immigration service she was finally successful in having the deportation order reversed, but technically she was guilty of kidnapping and defying Federal law.

This was typical of the bold way in which Donaldina operated: take the child and straighten out legalities later. Her technique was high-handed but often was the only effective way. Whoever had physical possession of the young girls had an important advantage no matter the justice of the case. This was attributable to the way in which the law operated at that time. Up until 1904 the procedures for obtaining legal custody even on a temporary basis were so cumbersome that had Donaldina followed the letter of the law many girls would simply have disappeared forever into a life of cruel degradation and physical suffering.

"In years past it was necessary in each case," Donaldina recalled, "to break the letter though not the spirit of the law when we rescued a Chinese child, for there was no written law to uphold us in entering a house and carrying off a child. Then, too, before it was possible to carry out guardianship proceedings, the ever available writ of habeus corpus would in many cases deliver the child back into the custody of the Chinese (slaver)."

Then, in 1904, Donaldina's attorney, at her instigation, succeeded in obtaining passage of a state law authorizing a presiding judge to have a child immediately taken by the local sheriff for temporary placement with applicants for guardianship. It was a breakthrough not only for Donaldina's work but in the entire field of child law.

Even after passage of the new law Donaldina still had to resort frequently to civil disobedience in order to prevent the return of a girl to slavery. She dodged writs, hid girls for whom warrants had been issued, and disobeyed court orders. Yet the more honest and compassionate judges, police and immigration officials remained her allies, chastising her when she bent the law but supporting her when they could.

This sporadic support was well-meant by the men who gave it and was actually courageous when it went against the graft-ridden government of San Francisco that abetted the slave trade. What is shocking is that there was no wide spread and uniform movement in San Francisco to abolish the entire slavery system. Over the decades tens of thousands of girls, as many as three thousand a year by some estimates, worked in the infamous crib and parlor houses of San Francisco's Chinatown.

Some who worked as prostitutes perhaps did so by choice but the vast majority were slaves in the trade. The system had its roots in the culture of homeland China where prostitution and slavery were open practices. But in America the slavery system of prostitution contravened the most essential aspect of law and was possible only through the continuing connivance of American officials who amassed fortunes in graft for winking at both the slave and opium trades.

Beyond the connivance of officialdom was the heartless indifference of society as a whole. Because of the prejudices of the times the Chinese girls were not real people to the white community people. What happened to them was of no real concern. In its lusty frontier character—alive into the 20th century—San Francisco took pride in its "sinfulness." There had always been wickedness in this city, after all, and the men of the town believed it their right to have a wild time on demand. The same spirit that spawned the topless bars of San Francisco in the 1960's nourished the slave trade of the 1860's and kept it alive for seventy years.

Unfortunately the few white women who took an interest in Donaldina's work shared something of the general prejudice against the Chinese. They were motivated in great part by their missionary zeal and a moral sense of superiority rather Puritan in character. The slave trade was, one suspects, a horror that they could point to in inspiring greater missionary zeal against a culture they deemed entirely depraved and misguided in its "paganism." A speech of one of Donaldina's supporters has survived that smacks loudly of "bearing the white man's burden" in saving the girls.

Although Donaldina may have shared some of the bias of her own church and mission orientation, her attitude toward her work and the Chinese people appears to have differed markedly from that of the other reformers who supported her refuge. Evidence of her respect for Chinese culture rests on the fact that the effectiveness of her work depended in large measure upon the trust and cooperation of a number of people in the Chinese community. Until fairly recent times and even now to some extent, San Francisco's Chinatown has been an extraordinarily closed community, run internally, policed internally, and distrustful of white interference. For Donaldina to have received information, for doors to have been unlocked, for her to have even survived without harm, there had to have been a network of Chinese with whom she enjoyed mutual regard and respect.

Evidence of her rapport with the Chinese is also found in the fact that her assistants at the home and in the conduct of the raids were themselves Chinese women. Indeed, as time progressed and the work of the home became more complex, various of these Chinese women themselves conducted raids to rescue others as they had once been rescued.

Perhaps the most convincing proof that Donaldina had regard for the Chinese culture is the frequency with which girls who entered the refuge were soon thereafter returned to China. Some, it is true were Anglicized first—becoming Christians as well as nurses and teachers— but an impressive number were returned to their homeland much as they had left it, to marry Chinese and assume a traditional Chinese life.

Of the girls who stayed with Donaldina at the refuge many learned not only domestic skills but trades as well. Among Donaldina's "daughters," one named Yoke Yeen became the first Chinese woman to graduate from Stanford University.

The slave trade continued in full force in San Francisco's Chinatown right up until the 1920's:

> It seems impossible that people made little or no protest against the vice and horror of the slave girls of Chinatown, so near the good cuisine at Marchands and the Poodle Dog. The early "scorchers" rushed by on the first bicycles in Golden Gate Park, the Gibson girls went boating on the ferryboat El Capitan singing "Bill Bailey, Won't You Please Come

Home." And the town remained docile, passive, and yet somehow uneasy over the inhumanity of actual slavery in a major American city.

In the 1920's a new police official pledged an end to the trade and set about the task with sincerity. Donaldina was now able to shift her efforts to other California cities, always keeping 920 Sacramento Street as home base.

In her forty-year career Donaldina rescued approximately three thousand girls. She retired from her work, principally that of rehabilitation in the later decades, in 1942. Leaving what had become "Cameron House," she moved to Palo Alto. In 1954 friends raised enough money to enable her to adopt a Korean orphan. Almost to the very end of her life she was "The Mother."

San Francisco's newspapers headlined her as "slave trade foe" and "mother who fought the tongs" and asserted that she had been marked for death a dozen times. But Donaldina long outlived her foes and the evil she fought. She died in Palo Alto in 1968 at the age of ninety-eight, a courageous woman whose long life bridged the closing of the frontier and the passing away of the last slavery in America.

6

Winning the Vote in the West

Esther Morris and Carrie Chapman Catt

We won't come in without our women
Wyoming Territorial Legislature

On September 6, 1870, the women of Wyoming went to the polls to cast their ballots. It was the first time that women anywhere in the world exercised the right to vote as fully enfranchised citizens.

What was particularly notable about this historic event was that it seemed to have happened in the wrong place and at the wrong time and for reasons that were not at all clear to those most concerned—the suffrage leaders in the East who had been laboring for thirty years unsuccessfully to get the vote for women. Another half century was to pass away before the lessons of Wyoming were understood in gaining the vote for women nationally.

By the time that the women of Wyoming were actually voting, the giants of the suffrage movement—Susan B. Anthony, Elizabeth Cady Stanton, Lucretia Mott and others—had spent three decades lecturing, petitioning, convening, and writing, but their tireless efforts had brought no tangible results. Far across the continent, however, in marked contrast, the vote for women in Wyoming came about quietly and in the comparative absence of what would today be termed "consciousness raising." There was virtually none of the continuing round of public speeches, rallies, and conventions that were so much a fixture of the woman's suffrage movement in the East. To all appearances there was not in Wyoming anything that could be called a woman's movement.

There was instead one remarkable woman: Esther Hobart McQuigg Slack Morris, the woman who became Wyoming's "Mother of Woman Suffrage." Standing six feet tall, weighing one hundred and

Carrie Chapman Catt *Photograph Courtesy of Sophia Smith Collection*

eighty pounds and having a "craggy countenance," Esther Morris
certainly didn't look like anyone's idea of the mother of anything, but
she virtually singlehandedly obtained the vote for Wyoming's women,
doing so with a direct political sense that was to elude the Eastern
suffragists for decades yet to come.

Esther Morris was born in Tioga County, New York, in 1813. She was one of a large family and when she was orphaned at age eleven she was apprenticed to a dressmaker. She subsequently met and married a railroad engineer named Artemus Slack in 1842 and the next year she bore a son who was named Edward. Three years later Slack died and Esther decided to move with her young son to pioneer Illinois to take up a tract of land that her husband had left her. But through her experience in Illinois with the injustice of property laws regarding women she became personally aware of the need for women's rights. Her commitment to human rights was furthered by her involvement at this time in the abolition movement.

In her new home of Peru, Illinois, Esther married a local merchant named John Morris. During the next twenty years she had three more sons (one dying in infancy) and was active in church work and civic causes. Then her husband and now-grown sons went to the boomtown of South Pass City, Wyoming, where a mining strike had attracted three thousand people almost overnight.

Esther went to Wyoming to join them in 1869. Her years in pioneer Illinois appear to have acclimated her to frontier life, for she took hold in Wyoming with notable speed, impressing her neighbors as "a born reformer." Within the year of her arrival she launched what was to be the first successful drive for woman suffrage in the country.

Her one-woman campaign though modest in scope was a minor classic in effective politics. Shortly before the first territorial election in the fall of 1869, she gave a tea party and invited two of the most promising politicians in the area. They were Democrat William H. Bright and Republican H. G. Nickerson, opponents for the same seat in the newly formed territorial legislature.

In the course of the party Esther extracted from each man the promise that, should he be elected, he would introduce a bill for woman suffrage. Tradition maintains that Democrat Bright gave his word to Esther because she had aided his wife during a difficult childbirth. With Bright supporting Esther's proposal Nickerson had to meet the challenge by matching his opponent's promise. Esther's timing in approaching both men while they were campaigning for election was excellent, and in securing the promise of each of them, she had in political parlance covered her bets.

As it turned out Bright won the seat in the territorial legislature and he kept his word to Esther Morris. In picking him as the one to carry her bill Esther had picked well; Bright not only won election but was chosen to head what was the equivalent of the territorial senate and thus was able to introduce the bill from a position of leadership and power.

The bill that Bright submitted on November 27, 1869, was simply worded for so momentous a matter. As *Council Bill Number 70* it read:

> Every woman of the age of twenty-one, residing in this Territory, may, at every election, cast her vote; and her right to the elective franchise and to hold office under the election laws of the Territory shall be the same as other electors.

Bright had little trouble securing passage of the bill by the Democratic-dominated legislature, and on December 10 the proposed law went to the governor for signature. One tradition maintains that the Democratic legislature passed the bill so readily because of an eagerness to embarrass the Republican governor by placing before him a highly controversial issue. If such were true, the legislators were deceived in their man. Almost immediately Governor John A. Campbell signed Council Bill Number 70 into law. He had, he said, once attended a conference on woman suffrage and had been impressed with the justice of the argument. To this extent the long campaign of the Eastern suffragists helped secure the landmark Wyoming victory.

Much of the rest of the nation immediately sat up and took notice of what had happened in the frontier territory:

> Tremendous publicity followed the enactment of the equal suffrage law. Wyoming was accused of passing "freak" legislation by opponents of the measure; was hailed by proponents as having passed the most forward-looking piece of legislation of the century.

The Wyoming legislators were apparently unperturbed by the reaction that was unfavorable. As companion legislation to the suffrage bill they enacted some of the most progressive measures on women's property rights in the nation. After her problems securing her property in Peru, Illinois, Esther Morris can be suspected of having had a hand in this later legislation as well as in the suffrage bill.

Although the rest of the country took note of Wyoming's bold step, oddly enough the woman suffragists in the East did not regard Esther's success in Wyoming as significant:

> In this bitter era of small achievement, it was strange that the one real victory passed almost unnoticed. Because it (Wyoming) was so remote—almost another country and almost uninhabited—the action did not seem important. The suffragists could not foresee that in the next years, the world's largest network of railways, tunneling through

mountain ranges and rushing across desert and vast distances, would
bind the nation together.

Undismayed that the national suffrage movement made little of their
breakthrough, the Wyoming women promptly took up their new
citizenship and began to enjoy its prerogatives.

Foremost among them, of course, was Esther Morris. On February
14, 1870, she accepted appointment as justice of the peace of South
Pass City. Not only was she the first woman to serve in such office in
the world, but the job she was given was a particularly challenging
one. South Pass City had a population of several thousand tough
miners, a handful of women, and a plentitude of saloons. Judge
Morris, as she was called, served well during her eight and a half
months in office. She herself viewed her unique position as "a test of
woman's ability to hold public office."

None of her judicial decisions were reversed on appeal, indicating
that they were sound. Of her other work as justice of the peace she said
in a rare interview:

> I have assisted in drawing a grand and petit jury, deposited a ballot and
> helped canvass the votes after the electing, and in performing all these
> duties I do not know as I have neglected my family any more than (in)
> ordinary shopping.

On her departure from office the *South Pass News* commended her
work: "Mrs. Justice Esther Morris retires from her judicial duties
today. She has filled the position with great credit to herself and
secured the good opinion of all with whom she has transacted any
official business."

During the period in which Esther Morris was serving as the world's
first justice of the peace, women of Laramie, Wyoming, were becoming the world's first to serve as jurors. As registered voters their names
were placed on the jury roles with the argument that women jurists
might be stern in applying the law, something heartily desired by a
community weary of violence going unpunished.

The Associated Press news service immediately wired the story all
over the nation that women were being impaneled as a jury. The
reaction was one of amusement and horror in the conservative Eastern
press. When Esther Morris had entered her job of justice of the peace,
Eastern papers had portrayed her as a cigar-smoking tough. Now
cartoonists and sketch artists from major periodicals flocked to
Laramie to produce similar caricatures of the women jurists. The
women responded by wearing veils, and the presiding judge assured

them that "you shall not be driven by the sneers, jeers and insults of a laughing crowd from the temple of justice, as your sisters have from some of the medical colleges of the land. The strong hand of the law shall protect you." He warned that it would be "a sorry day for any man who shall . . . by word or act endeavor to deter you from the exercise of those rights with which the law has invested you."

The cartoonists continued having a field day, and a number of jokes and ditties were widely circulated, one of them being:

> *Baby, baby don't get in a fury,*
> *Your mother's going to sit on a jury.*

The men of Wyoming continued to support women's active participation in politics despite the ridicule of the Eastern press. Nationally famous humorist Bill Nye, a resident of Wyoming from 1876 to 1883, wrote a sketch in which he pronounced woman suffrage "an unqualified success."

Twice, however, the important achievement of woman suffrage was brought into question in Wyoming. A repeal of the suffrage law was attempted in 1871 but failed. Then in 1890, when Wyoming sought entry into the Union as a state, the proposed state constitution's provision for woman suffrage brought serious opposition in Congress. The women of the state had organized for the purpose of being sure this provision was in the new state constitution sent by the legislature to Washington. Now that Congress was balking the women wired Wyoming's representative in Washington offering to have the suffrage provision removed and expressing confidence that the male voters of Wyoming would restore suffrage once Wyoming was accorded statehood. But another telegram, this one from the Wyoming legislature, was the one that prevailed: "We will remain out of the union a hundred years rather than come in without our women."

On March 28, 1890, admission of Wyoming to statehood with woman suffrage intact passed the House of Representatives narrowly while Susan B. Anthony and other leaders watched from the galleries. Three months later the Senate voted favorably, and the measure was signed by President Benjamin Harrison. The new state—the first to have full woman suffrage—celebrated entry into the union on July 23, 1890. On hand for the official celebration back home in Cheyenne was Esther Morris, chosen to present the flag of the occasion to the governor.

Over the ensuing years attempts were made to obtain woman suffrage in other territories and states in the West. So long as the effort was left in the hands of the Eastern suffrage leaders these attempts made little headway. One of the earliest efforts to win in the West had been made in Kansas in 1867. Two measures were proposed there, one enfranchising blacks and the other enfranchising women.

Confident of victory in a state to which many enlightened New Englanders had moved in the pre-Civil War days when reinforcements were needed to outvote pro-slavery settlers, the suffragist leaders descended on Kansas and started the usual round of speech-making.

Still smouldering with the hatred and bitterness of the days when it was "Bleeding Kansas," the state was a poor choice in 1867 for testing the questions of either black or woman suffrage. The Eastern campaigners made a gallant effort: Susan Anthony speaking in a half-finished church, Elizabeth Stanton trying to elude the prevalent bedbugs, Lucy Stone traveling up to forty miles a day in a springless wagon over rough Kansas roads. But the efforts were in vain. Woman suffrage lost the vote of the men of Kansas by an even bigger margin than did black suffrage.

The supposedly large base of local support had failed to materialize on its own. It would be many years before anyone in a position of national leadership would learn that victory in a state required a strong grass-roots organization within that state.

Sporadically over the years the Eastern leadership engaged in other forays into the West. Repeatedly these outside attempts failed, part of the reason being evident in the experiences of Susan Anthony and Anna Howard Shaw in South Dakota. Many years later Shaw recalled:

> That South Dakota campaign was one of the most difficult we ever made. It extended over nine months; and it is impossible to describe the poverty which prevailed throughout the whole rural community of the State. There had been three consecutive years of drought. The sand was like powder, so deep that the wheels of the wagons in which we rode "across country" sank half-way to the hubs; and in the midst of the dry powder lay withered tangles that had once been grass. Everyone had the foresaken, desperate look worn by the pioneer who has reached the limit of his endurance, and the great stretches of prairie roads showed innumerable canvas-covered wagons, drawn by starved horses, and followed by starved cows, on the way "Back East." Our talks with the despairing drivers of these wagons are among my most tragic memories.

Their talks with the despairing farmers of South Dakota could not have done much to advance the Great Cause. The frontier is no place to direct men's minds to woman suffrage when their faces are set eastward in defeat and the promise of the frontier has fled before three years of drought.

The failure to consider local conditions, to strategize state by state, to build grass-roots organizations, to develop an overall campaign plan—all this continued to hamstring the woman's suffrage movement for decades. No one at the national level seemed able to arrive at the political sense demonstrated by Esther Morris in Wyoming. She had picked her time well—the moment before a new government (and attitudes along with it) coalesced. She had picked her specific goal—a bill to enfranchise women. She had picked her target—men standing for election and eager for support.

By contrast the national leaders did not use good timing but let territory after territory pass from the fluid stage of frontier attitudes into more conservative stance. Similarly, they did not concentrate on a specific goal but persisted in mixing the woman suffrage question with temperance, unionism, and other causes and thereby multiplied their enemies. Further they were negligent in choosing wisely their immediate targets of support; theirs was the shotgun method that expended energies and talents gallantly but wastefully.

Yet enfranchisement of women in the West continued to expand despite failure at the national level of the movement. For a bleak fifty years the successes in the West were the only ones on the suffrage map. In 1893 Colorado became the second state in the union to enact woman suffrage. Three years later Idaho followed suit. Then came Utah in 1896. At the end of the century only four states, all of them in the West, were in the suffrage ranks.

Fourteen years went by after Utah before there were any more suffrage states and then, when they came with a rush, they were all in the West: California in 1911; Arizona, Kansas, and Oregon in 1912; Alaska in 1913; and Nevada and Montana in 1914. Almost three-quarters of a century after the woman's suffrage movement began, the only areas where women were full citizens were in the West.

That the West looked favorably upon enfranchising women was undoubtedly due to the frontier conditions that prevailed or had prevailed. It was hard for men to deny the vote to women who had handled weapons, braved the overland trail, starved and struggled alongside the men or on their own against all manner of conditions.

As basic perhaps as the respect that women had won on the frontier was the high value that they had assumed in the eyes of men when their numbers were scarce during the pioneer period. This veneration toward women in the West continued long after the numbers of the sexes began to even out. Their relatively sparse numbers also made them seem less of a threat at the polls to men, a common argument of the day being that if women were enfranchised they would vote as a block against males.

There is also a possibility that men in the West, engaged as they were in such elemental tasks as mining, bronc-busting, and lumbering, felt more confident of their essential masculinity and therefore did not feel so threatened by the prospect of women having an equal voice in political affairs.

The victories in the West were attributable to these factors in a general way, but in several of the earliest wins there were particular circumstances at work. One of these involved a conflict in women's rights, and the others centered on the talents of a Western woman who, like Esther Morris, had basic political sense.

In the first case, that of Utah, woman suffrage was used as a political weapon by both sides in the conflict between Mormons and non-Mormons over the question of polygamy. Believing that Mormon women would, if enfranchised, vote to prohibit polygamy, an Indiana Congressman introduced a bill in Washington in 1869 to give Utah women the right to vote. The Mormons in Utah realized that the Indiana Congressman's basic assumption was wrong—Mormon women obeyed their church and were held in bondage in polygamy by religious conviction and not by lack of political power. Confident that their women would not use the ballot against the church, the Utah legislature turned the tables on Washington and voted in 1870 to allow women of the territory to vote.

It was an astute move, permitting the Mormons to claim that they were truly egalitarian toward women, polygamy notwithstanding. Further, the enfranchisement of their women substantially increased the number of Mormon voters at a time when the Mormons were struggling to maintain their political power in the face of a growing number of non-Mormon settlers in Utah.

Ignorant of the politics of the state, a number of suffrage leaders in the East now looked with friendly eyes upon Mormony. As a consequence, the champion against polygamy, Ann Eliza Young, found herself being attacked in the women's rights press for taking issue with the Mormons. To suffragists in the East, the right to vote outweighed even the obnoxious condition of polygamy.

For fourteen years the women of Utah voted—but only according to church dictates, Ann Eliza and others claimed. Then Congress took away the franchise as a punitive measure against Utah for defiantly maintaining polygamy. As a result the women of Utah were twice punished, being left in polygamy and now without suffrage. In 1893, after Mormon leaders finally renounced polygamy, the territory was permitted to enter the Union as a state and with woman suffrage restored.

The other two early suffrage victories in the West that are significant were those in Idaho and Colorado. It was in the campaigns in these two states that there emerged a woman whose political talents would eventually permeate the national suffrage movement and play a major part in securing passage of the Constitutional amendment that finally crowned the long suffrage effort.

Carrie Lane Chapman Catt was born in Wisconsin and moved to Iowa as a youngster. After graduating from Iowa State College she taught school, worked as a school administrator, and then went into journalism, first in Iowa and then in San Francisco. Her first marriage ended tragically with the sudden death of her husband only a few months after the wedding. To fill the gap in her life Carrie started lecturing and working on behalf of woman suffrage in Iowa. The women of the state were organized into an effective network and, although the temperance question repeatedly blocked their efforts to win suffrage, they demonstrated to Carrie the value of organization.

Her efforts in Iowa drew the attention of national leaders and she was asked to help in the South Dakota campaign of 1890. After being exposed to the same kind of disheartening experiences that Anna Shaw and Susan Anthony encountered in the plains state, Carrie was convinced that barnstorming through sparsely settled regions was of little value and that the absence of a grass-roots organization was fatal.

Carrie had meantime married George Catt, a wealthy engineer who was a strong supporter of woman suffrage, but after the South Dakota debacle, she pulled back from active involvement. Then in 1893 the women of Colorado asked her for her help in passing a referendum on woman suffrage. Encouraged by the fact that the women of the state had already organized themselves, Carrie agreed to participate.

The victory in Colorado that year, the first to be achieved by popular vote, was due to various causes, among them the complacency of the opposition in assuming the measure was doomed. But a great deal of the credit goes to Carrie. Not only did she contribute in terms of her speaking and organizational abilities, but she gave to the male population an example of woman's "grit" that was influential in winning support to the cause. The incident that became known as Carrie's "wild ride" occurred in the mountains of Colorado when a wrecked train blocked her journey to her next speaking engagement. Rather than accept the delay, Carrie rode a handcar all by herself, careening around mountain curves through the night with her hat pinned firmly to her head and a bag of sandwiches at her feet.

As colorful as was the wild ride, what happened in her next campaign was even more significant. In Idaho in 1896 Carrie participated in the first effort in which suffragists were organized to work precinct by precinct in turning out a vote favorable to a referendum on woman suffrage. The measure passed in Idaho and the method became the one that Carrie would apply twenty-one years later on the national level in the critical battle to win New York State, a battle she led and won.

In 1895 Carrie was made chairman of a newly established Organization Committee in Washington after she castigated the national suffrage convention for the failure to plan and organize. She was a visionary who brought from the West the techniques that had long been missing but would finally bring success to the movement nationally.

In giving Carrie Chapman Catt to the movement the West contributed a great talent to the national effort. And when the showdown came on voting for the long-sought Constitutional amendment the Congressmen and Senators of the West from suffrage states were critical to passage of the amendment. Fifty years after Wyoming led the way, women throughout America were finally enfranchised.

Then, in the East, the woman's rights movement faltered. Having won the vote the national leaders retired from the scene instead of going on to active political careers. Afraid that they might be accused of having sought their own ends in promoting suffrage, the talented and capable women who had led the fight nationally dropped their activities and allowed the energies and organization to dissipate.

In the West, however, women had no such hesitancy. Jeanette Rankin, the first Congresswoman, was elected in 1916 from Montana. Years later Congress was voting on America's entry into World War II, and she cast the sole dissenting vote. (In 1958 John F. Kennedy included her as one of "Three Women of Courage" in a magazine article he authored, and in 1968 she was back in Washington leading a peace march against the Vietnam War.)

The West was also the first to elect other women to public office. Among them were Nell Ross of Wyoming, first woman governor and later Director of the Mint. The nation's second woman governor was also from the West: Miriam "Ma" Ferguson of Texas.

The remarkable pioneer Esther Morris was not forgotten in the state that led the way in opening politics to women. In 1960, fifty-eight years after her death at the age of eighty-seven, she was officially designated the *Mother of Woman Suffrage* by the state of Wyoming and statues of her were placed in the state's capitol and in Statuary Hall in Washington.

Carrie Chapman Catt did not seek political office herself but in 1920 she spoke perceptively of what lay ahead for newly enfranchised women, urging them to go beyond the ballot and to the "locked door" of real political power. "You will have a long hard fight before you get behind that door, for there is the engine that moves the wheels of your party machinery . . . If you really want women's votes to count, make your way there."

Ann Eliza Young

I felt a new impulse stirring within me which made me strong
Ann Eliza Young

A Wife of Brigham Young Fights Polygamy
After a person has made up his or her mind to take any step in a new direction, it seems as though every event of life points the same way. It is almost as if the decision had been forced upon him and the course of action was inevitable.

So reflected Ann Eliza Young in her book *Wife No. 19 or The Story of a Life in Bondage.* She wrote of the last moments before she set upon a course of action that was eventually to be a significant factor in the official abolishment of polygamy among the Mormons, and the end of one of the most degrading and painful conditions ever imposed upon women in America.

At this moment of decision Ann Eliza had resolved to leave her husband Brigham Young, head of the Mormon Church and the prophet of the Mormon people. This decision would, she knew, wrench her away forever from family and friends, shatter her commitment to the religion she had been raised in, and cast her out into a world of strangers, the "gentiles" she had been taught to hate and fear. Her action against Young might also, for all she knew, place her in danger of her very life, for she was now pitting herself against one of the most determined and powerful men in America and the system that protected him and his prerogatives.

Oddly enough the cataclysmic struggle she was about to undertake was triggered specifically by the small matter of a cookstove. She had gone to her husband's office to ask him for money for the stove so that she might better serve the boarders she had taken in. It was her position that the boarders were necessary in order for her to support herself and her children, something that Brigham Young, despite his millions, had failed to do. Young had agreed to her original proposal to take in gentile boarders but he now refused to provide money for the stove. For Ann Eliza, as she faced the aging, white-haired prophet, this was the last straw. After five years of the ignonimies of plural marriage, Ann Eliza had had enough. She left Young's office and, in the course of her walk home, decided to leave him and seek the protection of gentiles she had met through her boarders.

She was an unlikely rebel, born the daughter of two of the earliest converts to Mormonism, her father and mother having followed founder Joseph Smith through the terrible persecutions in Ohio, then Missouri, and finally Illinois, where Smith met death at the hands of a gentile mob. When the Mormons undertook their epic overland crossing to a new homeland in Utah under their new leader Brigham Young, Ann Eliza's family was among them. Her earliest memories were actually of the arduous trek to the desert sanctuary. (For her at age two the journey was a delight.)

There were other of Ann Eliza's childhood memories that were, however, not so pleasant. "I often wonder if there is a child in Mormondom born under the blight of polygamy, who knows what it is to have a happy, joyous childhood, rendered more happy and more joyous by the smiling, calm content of the mother . . . " Of her own mother's situation, she wrote: "I never remember on her face one such look as I see daily upon mother's faces now . . . I came to her when the greatest misery of her life was about to fall upon her; and that misery came to her as it came to all the (Mormon) women then, under the guise of religion—something that must be endured 'for Christ's sake.' And, as her religion had brought her nothing but persecution and sacrifice, she submitted to this new trial as to everything that had preceded it, and she received polygamy as a cross laid upon her."

As Ann Eliza watched her mother struggle to bear this cross, she developed the deepest aversion to this peculiar institution of Mormonism. Of all the tenets of the Mormon faith, polygamy was the most controversial. Instituted in the 1840's by Joseph Smith, it was not publicly announced until a decade later by Brigham Young, Smith's successor, although it was practiced in the intervening years by the Mormon leadership. Indeed there was great pressure on the leaders second to Smith and Young to adopt the practice that many Mormon males initially felt was repugnant.

Eliza's own father was among those pressured to enter polygamy, and he and his wife wrestled long with the problem. He was a less devout Mormon than she but one determined to succeed within the Mormon economic structure. "He and my mother had many a long, tearful talk over it; and although they received the doctrine, believing it must be right, they could not for some time make up their minds to put it into practice."

Smith's death in Illinois gave the couple a respite from pressure to enter polygamy but, upon succeeding Smith, Young soon took up "counseling" the couple. At last they acquiesed and took into their marriage a second wife.

One of the characteristics of Mormon polygamy was the way in which the leaders relentlessly pushed it upon their fellows. So shocking was the doctrine originally to even Mormons that apparently those who wished to practice polygamy felt they could do so only with widespread adoption among their co-religionists.

If polygamy shocked the rank and file of Mormons when they first heard of it, it positively outraged their gentile neighbors. Throughout the West women were scarce and much of the antagonism for the Mormons after they reached Utah undoubtedly arose from the basic resentment of womenless frontier men confronted with a system in which one man had several wives.

The question then remains as to how women were lured into polygamy when the frontier offered so many single or widowed men. The answer lies at least partially in an ingenious system of supply and distribution that was a by-product of the Mormon's continuing recruitment of new followers. Ceaselessly the Mormon elders sent missionaries out into the world to seek new converts for "the gathering of Zion." Cannily, they fastened on England as a principle target just at the time when the Industrial Revolution had uprooted thousands upon thousands of English people from rural and village life. To the dispossessed and impoverished lower classes now thrust into the horrors of mid-19th century factory and sweat shop, the message of salvation brought by the Mormons must have appeared to be a dual one: eternal bliss in heaven and a much-improved material existence in faraway Utah.

People from the British Isles—among them thousands of young women cut adrift from their rural families—enlisted in the new religion. Once proselytized, the converts were carefully herded by a chain of missionaries over the ocean by ship, past the temptations of the East Coast cities, and then across the wide empty plains and mountains to the desert fastness of Utah. Many young British women did not know what lay ahead of them. When they reached Salt Lake it was literally too late to turn back or to resist. Friendless and poor in a desert land, they were in a real sense trapped. To many an impoverished woman in the wilderness, polygamy must have seemed the lesser of evils.

Although there was a strong element of entrapment in the foregoing, the web that predominantly ensnared women into polygamy was far more subtle, being the one that caught Ann Eliza's mother. "My mother often said that the 'Revelation' (of polygamy as a heaven-decreed doctrine) was the most hateful thing in the world to her, and she dreaded and abhorred it, but she was afraid lest she be found 'fighting against the Lord.'" Religious devotion—blind and submissive—was what basically drew women into subjecting themselves to a condition that was for most of them heartbreaking.

A number of the women who came to Salt Lake in the early years did so by handcart rather than by wagon, pulling their possessions and food supplies across the long miles of rugged terrain. When Brigham Young devised this cheaper method of transportation he appointed Ann Eliza's father to oversee the building of the carts. Subsequently, when the handcart experiment broke down and hundreds of exhausted and starving converts were stranded en route to Salt Lake, he was commissioned to go back and help in the rescue effort.

Shortly he went even further and rescued several handcart women from destitution by marrying them. It was typical of Mormon men that the inner struggle over taking plural wives ended after the first plural marriage. Ann Eliza noted bitterly the readiness with which her father took a third, fourth, and fifth wife. As for Ann Eliza's mother, she had literally passed beyond caring. "The hurt comes with the first plural wife; no suffering can ever exceed the pain she feels then." This time it was the second wife who felt betrayed and hurt.

Ann Eliza herself never intended to enter into plural marriage nor had she anything but distaste for the common practice of elderly Mormon men in taking wives a fraction of their age. But if ever a woman was trapped into polygamous marriage it was Ann Eliza.

After her first marriage to a man named John Dee ended in divorce, Ann Eliza went to her parents' farm, content to raise her two sons by Dee and to enjoy the peace that followed the stormy relationship with her former husband. She had not been at the farm long when Brigham Young came as an honored visitor. He was attracted to the strikingly beautiful divorcee. He queried her on her future plans regarding remarriage and strongly urged her to consider such despite her repeated replies that she was perfectly happy as she was. Young spoke to her in a fatherly way in the guise of a counselor but, upon leaving her, he immediately went to her parents to request her in marriage.

Ann Eliza's parents were now in an extemely difficult position. They were torn between obeying their spiritual leader and respecting Ann Eliza's feelings. And she was emphatic that she did not want to marry Brigham Young.

Before long she found that it was not easy to reject a man who was not only a spiritual leader but a temporal dictator as well. Her brother had recently entered into a business contract with Brigham Young, and when the enterprise failed, Young threatened to ruin him and drive him from the church. Ann Eliza's entire family, particularly her devout brother, were in agony of spirit.

Then Young let it be known that the whole matter would be forgotten if Ann Eliza would consent to marry him. In order to spare her brother and his family expulsion from the church, Ann Eliza gave in.

Young sweetened the transaction by offering to provide her a thousand dollars as a wedding gift and a house of her own, the latter being something Ann Eliza insisted on in order to avoid living with the multitude of other wives.

Ann Eliza never received the thousand dollars and the house Young provided her was small and ill-furnished. Further, food and clothing were in short supply. Ann Eliza was also annoyed by the fact that Brigham Young, after literally forcing her into marriage, never gave her his company exclusively on outings. Then, as if in punishment for the dissatisfactions she expressed to him, he ordered Ann Eliza to take over management of his farm outside Salt Lake. The burden of work wore her down and almost killed her mother who had come to help her serve the "Lion of the Lord."

When the farm stay ended and Ann Eliza returned to Salt Lake, Young told her that she would have to send her mother away because he could not afford to support her. This seemed outrageous to Ann Eliza after the work that her mother had done for Young, but he held to his position and Ann Eliza had to find money to repay Young for her mother's board. It was thus that she came to the decision that she would have to earn money for herself and her family by taking in boarders.

Now when Young refused to help her even so much as in the matter of the cookstove, Ann Eliza reached the decision that she had agonized over for a long time. As soon as she got home after confronting Young, she arranged to have her older son sent to stay with relatives some distance from Salt Lake. Next she had the furniture in the house removed and sold, netting three hundred dollars as a meager nest egg with which to face an uncertain future.

Before Young realized what was happening, Ann Eliza had not only left him but had enlisted the help of some of her new gentile friends who immediately sheltered her and her younger son in the Walker House, Salt Lake's leading gentile hotel.

As the first long night of her new life dragged by, Ann Eliza lay awake in her hotel room, terror growing in her that Brigham Young would seek violent revenge. She had not only defied him but had joined forces with the hated gentiles. She had heard stories of the fate of other apostates from Mormonism, of the fallaways who were found dead on the roads leading from Salt Lake. The stories seemed very real to Ann Eliza as she lay sleepless and afraid in her little hotel room.

But the night finally passed and Ann Eliza remained firm in her decision. No matter what might happen she would not go back to Brigham Young.

The new day brought a new dimension to her situation. Suddenly she was an exciting news item and she was besieged almost immediately by newspapermen seeking interviews with the woman who had dared walk out on the mighty Brigham.

The resulting headline stories across the country brought an offer to Ann Eliza from one of the nation's leading lecture bureaus to take her story directly to the people in person. This initial offer was set aside but it was not forgotten by one of her new gentile friends.

Meantime Ann Eliza fought to make sense of her position. She was fearful for her life and felt herself to be virtually a prisoner in the Walker House, afraid even to go to the dining room for her meals. She had no sense of what her future would be. And her past tugged at her in a most distressing way. From her mother came a letter in which the woman who had suffered grievously under polygamy, begged her daughter to return to it.

> You can never know how dear you are to me your grief-striken mother. Your death would have been far preferrable to the course you are taking. How gladly would I have laid you in your grave, had I known what was in your heart. I now pray that you may be spared for repentance and atonement, for as sure as you are living, a day of repentance will come, a day of reckoning and sorrow such as you have never imagined.

One phrase in the letter underscored what was held by the Mormons to be Ann Eliza's principle sin: her mother urged her to "flee from your present dictators as you would from the fiends of darkness." In the eyes of her family and of the Mormon community, Ann Eliza had obviously become the dupe of the archenemy of all Mormonry. It was incomprehensible to them that she was acting out of her own choice and not from the influence of her gentile "dictators."

But Ann Eliza was not the dupe of the gentiles. She had a very clear sense of who the real dictators in her life had been, and as perilous as freedom was, she not only clung to it with determination but began to think about fighting to free other women still enslaved in polygamy. Slowly her future role began to take shape in her mind. Her plan began modestly enough when she was asked by others staying in the hotel to address a small gathering of the guests on the story of her experience.

Feeling somewhat protected from Mormon vengeance by the publicity she had received, Ann Eliza ventured down from her room to speak to the group assembled. "I stood for a moment gazing in sudden bewilderment; the blood rushed to my face, and my first impulse was to run away and hide myself in my room."

But she overcame her fear and spoke to the people before her of how she had come to be among them. When she was finished she "saw tears on more than one cheek."

The experience reinforced her determination to build a life for herself. "I felt able to take care of myself and my children, if I could see a way to do it. I was not afraid to work, and I felt a new impulse stirring within me which made me strong. Life was my own and I would do the best I could."

The experience of speaking to the assemblage in the Walker House opened a new road for her. The offer of a job as lecturer was recalled, but instead of signing on with the lecture bureau, Ann Eliza accepted the suggestion of one of her gentile friends that he become her manager. He immediately set to work booking her into public halls in cities from Laramie to Boston.

There yet remained the problem of getting her safely out of Utah. A plan was devised for sneaking her out of the Walker House a day ahead of her announced departure. Next, she was to board an eastbound train at a flagstop far outside Salt Lake just at dawn. Her father came forward to aid in her escape, an action that argues for the fact that she was in real physical danger. "The night was intensely dark . . . and as we plunged on through the night, we were a gloomy and apprehensive party. We were not sure how closely we had been watched, or whether we had succeeded in eluding Mormon vigilance.''

Twice they got lost in the dark Utah countryside, but at last they reached the train stop. When Ann Eliza boarded the train at dawn, she was at first exhilarated at being safely on her way and then was overcome with ''such utter loneliness that, for a moment, I was bewildered by the situation.''

She turned to her traveling companion, a Mrs. Cooke, and asked, ''What shall I do?''

''Keep up a brave heart and think of the work before you,'' was the reply.

Ann Eliza followed this advice and for the next ten years as she lectured from coast to coast, she never lost sight of her work and her commitment to end polygamy. For a decade she lectured full time against the evils of Mormon plural marriage, working nine months out of twelve, year after year. While her two sons were cared for in a home she provided for them, she traveled a ceaseless round of faceless hotel rooms. Hers was a wearing existence of badly cooked meals, drab railroad stations, and uncomfortable trains. But she was doing what she had set out to do, providing a living for herself and her children and at the same time fighting against polygamy.

Wherever she went, whether large city, small town, frontier village or the nation's capital, her message was always the same: polygamy must be ended through the vigorous action of the United States government. She met with members of Congress, wrote to successive presidents over a decade and to their wives. Always she pleaded that action be taken to free her sisters still in bondage.

Her impact in rallying public opinion against polygamy was not only effective, but she herself became a successful lecturer, earning remarkably high fees for the time. Not only was her material sensational in itself but her impassioned delivery, her personal beauty, and her developing stage presence made Ann Eliza a star of the lecture circuit.

Yet it was a difficult road that she traveled. Added to the loneliness of being separated from her children and the exhaustion of a life of ceaseless travel was the long fight involved in divorcing Young and in combatting the smear campaign that began not long after she left Utah.

The worst of the smear attacks consisted of charges placed in a midwestern newspaper that Ann Eliza and her manager had been seen entering the same hotel rooms and Pullman berths. Ann Eliza and her friends were successful in refuting the slander but for a short time her entire career seemed imperiled.

The smear not only failed but produced a result that was truly a happy one from Ann Eliza's point of view. Her mother was so scandalized by the smear attempt against Ann Eliza that she finally chose her daughter over Mormonism, left Utah, and came to live in Ann Eliza's home.

Under mounting public pressure, much of it fueled by Ann Eliza's campaign, Congress began to move against polygamy. It was difficult to write laws that would be effective in enforcement and there was also a great deal of opposition to any laws prohibiting polygamy because of the constitutional question as to whether such laws were an infringement of religious freedom. But at last a strong bill was enacted in 1882 and polygamy was doomed.

For some eight years the Mormons struggled to keep polygamy alive. Men with plural wives were known as "cohabs" and cohab hunts" by federal officers who kept Mormon men on the run. Life was extremely difficult during this period for polygamous families, with many wives left to forge for themselves and children placed under the stigma of illegitimacy.

Finally in 1890, with Mormon families scattered and broken and with the determination of the Federal government persisting, the Mormon leadership capitulated. An agreement was signed by the Mormon leaders prohibiting any future plural marriages and, in exchange, the Federal government agreed to legitimatize the children of existing polygamous marriages and to end the cohab hunts. Though Mormon families were now left unmolested to continue existing polygamous relationships, there would be no more plural marriages. Fifty years after its institution by Joseph Smith, polygamy was dead.

Monogamous marriage, which Ann Eliza had fought to uphold, did not itself prove a boon to her. In 1883 she retired from the lecture circuit and married Moses R. Denning, a wealthy Michigan timberman. Denning had divorced his wife of twenty-five years when he fell in love with Ann Eliza, but the new love did not last. Ann Eliza charged in a subsequent divorce action that Denning had carried on with house servants and other women after marrying her.

Other tragedies came to Ann Eliza in the years after she retired from lecturing. One of her sons died of tuberculosis in early adulthood and at about the same time Ann Eliza's mother died. And although Ann Eliza had actually lectured in Utah during her anti-polygamy campaign, she remained forever estranged from her father and the rest of her family.

Her book, *Wife No. 19,* written in 1875, had been a great success, but a second book, written in 1909 when she was undoubtedly in great need of money, failed dismally. The subject of polygamy no longer was of public interest and the thousand copies of *A Life in Bondage,* printed at Ann Eliza's own expense, did not sell.

At this point Ann Eliza completely disappeared from view. What became of her, where and when she died, are questions that historians have been unable to answer. A tradition among her descendants is that she died in abject poverty in the East and was buried in a pauper's field. It was a sad ending for so beautiful and gallant a woman. Even more regrettable is the fact that she has received little credit for the work she did in fighting polygamy. Most of the commentary on Ann Eliza has been written either by male historians or by female descendants of Brigham Young. Among the former there is a strong tendency to dismiss Ann Eliza as a "shrew" because of the invective she directed against Young. Young's female descendants have, on the other hand, taken the position that she was a scheming woman who sought to exploit the fact of her marriage to Young and that this, rather than opposition to polygamy, actually motivated her lecture career.

In reality, however, polygamy was a heartbreaking and degrading condition for women and, for her long fight against it, the lecture fees that Ann Eliza earned were scant reward. Suffering poverty and loneliness in her last years, Ann Eliza had satisfaction only in the fact that she had indeed kept up a good heart and thought of the work before her.

Bright Eyes La Flesche

An Indian Woman Fights for Justice

We are here now, but for how long?
Chief Joseph of the Omahas

Joseph Iron Eyes La Flesche, chief of the Omaha Indians dictated these words to his daughter, Bright Eyes, as she wrote a letter for him in 1876: "Look ahead and you will see nothing but the white man, the future is full of the white man, and we shall be as nothing before him."

By that year the Western frontier had almost completely closed upon the Indian tribes of the Great Plains. The last tribal buffalo hunt had been held two years before with scant results, and white settlers were steadily encroaching on the Indian lands pledged in perpetuity to the Omaha tribe by the United States government.

The decade that followed Iron Eyes' letter was the decade of sorrow on the plains as the buffalo Indians struggled against decimation by the whites. It was in most respects a hopeless fight and the Omahas, under Joseph's guidance avoided open conflict. Each instance of Indian resistance or retaliation only provided the whites with an excuse for vicious reprisals, and the massacres and removal of other plains tribes in these years became one of the most shameful episodes in the history of the nation.

Yet in this decade of darkness Bright Eyes was to become a young Indian woman who could fight the whites bloodlessly and effectively, using against them the weapons of their own culture.

Bright Eyes, the eldest daughter of Chief Iron Eyes, was born in 1854 near today's Bellview, Nebraska. Her father, the son of a white fur trader and an Indian mother, had been adopted as a young man by the Omaha chief whom he succeeded in authority. Iron Eyes' experience with the world of the whites convinced him that his people could survive the impending destruction of the Indian world only by educating their children in white culture, adopting agriculture, and resisting the temptation to go to war against the ever-pressing white people.

Iron Eyes was successful in keeping his people at peace with the whites and in keeping alcohol off the Omaha lands. He also persuaded his people to adopt agriculture and he sent all of his children, Bright Eyes among them, to a nearby school established by missionaries. Going to the white school, dressing as a white, and submitting to white lifestyle was an excruciating experience for Bright Eyes and the other Indian children caught in the cultural shift.

Upon completion of schooling under the missionaries, Bright Eyes had a desire to learn more. Through the help of a sympathetic teacher, she became one of the first plains Indians to receive more than the skimpy education offered by the little missionary schools. At the age of seventeen she departed for New Jersey to enter Elizabeth Institute.

Graduating with honors, Bright Eyes returned to the Omaha reservation anticipating that she would now be able to serve her people as a teacher. But the door was shut to her. Repeatedly and unsuccessfully she implored the local Indian agent and the Indian Affairs Commission in Washington to hire her as a teacher.

The local agent insisted that there were no teaching positions available at the Omahas' school and even though half of the Omaha children were going without schooling because of inadequate facilities, he refused to permit the Indians' own funds to be used for construction of a second school. As for the Indian Commission, Bright Eyes did not so much as receive a reply to her letters.

Two years went by as Bright Eyes continued to seek an opportunity to make use of her education for the benefit of her tribe. Added to her own disheartening situation were the hardships that fell upon her people during this period. Having committed themselves to an agricultural life, the Omahas were now vulnerable to the misfortunes that can befall farmers. During the good crop years they had been unable to accumulate a reserve because all of their farm produce had to be sold through the Indian agent at the low prices he set. When the bad crop years came the Omahas could not even fall back upon hunting, since the game that they had relied upon in the past had disappeared with the coming of the white people.

The Omahas and the educated Bright Eyes went hungry. What relief supplies were sent by the government found their way into the hands of the friends of the Indian agent, a common occurrence within the graft-ridden "Indian Ring" of the period.

While the Omahas suffered hunger and injustice on their Nebraska lands, the plains Indian farther west were being totally stripped of their lands and rounded up on reservations despite treaties previously sworn to by the federal government. In 1876 the Sioux retaliated, wiping out General George Custer and his men at the Little Bighorn River in a climax of resistance. But the victory of battle was not a real victory. The plains Indians were hunted down and relocated, suffering terrible hardships as they attempted to flee through the fierce winter of the Northern Plains. In this aftermath of the Little Bighorn, Chief Iron Eyes' policy of non-combativeness seemed to be wise in spite of the hardships the Omahas were undergoing.

It was at this same time, 1877, that Bright Eyes first began in a small way to utilize a technique for fighting the whites that was far more effective than warfare. In essence what she did was to use the tactics of the system she was fighting. Looking carefully through the government regulations pertaining to Indian affairs, she found a rule stating that Indians were to be given preference over whites in the granting of jobs in the Indian Service. She wrote to the Indian Commission citing this regulation and threatening that if it were not honored she would take her case to the newspapers:

> It's all a farce when you say you are trying to civilize us, then, after we educate ourselves, refuse us positions of responsibility and leave us utterly powerless to help ourselves. Perhaps the only way to make ourselves heard is to appeal to the American public through the press. They might listen.

At one stroke Bright Eyes had hit upon a classic way to manipulate the American political system. Not only was she turning one part of the system against another—citing official regulations in the face of their abuse by officials—but she was threatening to enlist powerful political levers in the form of publicity in the press and the stirring of public opinion. Response to her threat was prompt. Suddenly, although it was at half pay, she had the teaching job she had sought so long.

It is likely that she hit upon these techniques inadvertently, although her letter is worded with great confidence. In any event her new found tactics were not only effective but represented a potential breakthrough for the Indians in dealing with a government heretofore callous to their straightforward pleading. Although the stakes in this one incident were by some standards small, being one job for one Indian woman, the victory for that one woman was great and the way had been pointed out by which the Omahas could fight more effectively than the Sioux and other tribes at war with the whites.

Bright Eyes' victory and its implications for the future were, however, overshadowed by tragic news that came to the Omahas concerning the closely related Ponca tribe. Though the Poncas, like the Omahas, had remained patient with white abuses and never acted in hostile fashion, the government had ordered the tribe removed to Indian Territory, that barren land (in what would one day be Oklahoma) where malaria and change of climate were deadly to the northern tribes.

The Poncas and Omahas were so closely allied by blood ties and intermarriage that the removal of the former literally meant the division of families. For the Omahas the blow was as heavy as if it had fallen directly upon their own tribe.

Without resistance the Poncas left their recently built homes, their tools and livestock, and the crops that stood in their newly established fields. After years of hard work in adopting the ways of white people, the Poncas were arbitrarily wrenched from their homeland and deprived of all their possessions. Though they departed peacefully, they were marched away under army guard.

There was great bitterness among both tribes and much of it was directed at Chief Iron Eyes. Under his counsel they had given over their Indian culture and, in effect, waged the loss of their age-old lifestyle and their identity as a people on the reliability of the whites.

The Ponca's journey to Indian Territory was virtually a death march. The army record kept en route noted stop after stop being made for the purpose of conducting burials. At the end of the long, sorrowful trek, the Poncas were abandoned without food, shelter or tools in an inhospitable land.

The Omahas were not only grief-stricken at the fate of their relatives, but fearful that the same future would soon be theirs. Like the Poncas they had been peaceful toward the whites and tractable. Time and again they, like the Poncas, had ceded land to the whites without violent protest. They too had tried to adapt to the ways of the whites and had established farms and built houses as had the Poncas. None of this had forestalled injustice to the Poncas and the Omahas now believed that nothing would prevent similar treatment being dealt to them.

Worst of all was the realization that the Poncas had had a treaty with the government granting them their land forever. If such a treaty could not save the Poncas, it could not save the Omahas.

For Bright Eyes this period must have been an especially painful one. Her Ponca relatives had been driven away, her father's policies and leadership were in serious question, and the removal of her own tribe was a real possibility. Perhaps worst of all, as a teacher in a school oriented to the white culture she had to teach America's ideals of human rights and justice to Indian children denied them. Furthermore, she was not only in the position of having to give voice to what was for the Indians a hollow promise, but she was also an integral part of the process of moving the children mentally and psychologically into the white world where, unlike the Indian world, aspirations lived on paper instead of in actions.

Then, in 1879, events occurred which led Bright Eyes away from the role of schoolteacher and to that of leadership in fighting injustice. In that year, at the juncture of the Arkansas and Salt Fork Rivers in Indian Territory, malaria swept through the Ponca tribe killing a large percentage of the people, among them the sixteen-year-old son of Standing Bear, one of the tribal chiefs. Before his death the young man made his father promise to bury him in the northern home of the tribe. Death had by this time taken two hundred and eighty of the seven hundred Poncas whom the government had originally driven south. With the death of Standing Bear's son, all of the chief's children had perished except one small daughter. Standing Bear's forebearance was at an end. He loaded his son's body on a wagon and, with about thirty followers, Standing Bear headed for home.

The little band of men, women and children struggled north through the winter over hundreds of miles of storm-swept prairie. No sooner had they arrived at their homeland than they were rounded up by the Army under orders from Washington for removal once again to the dreaded Indian Territory.

In vain the Omahas pleaded for the people of their sister tribe. They offered, as they had offered at the time of the first removal, to share their lands with the Poncas. The pleas were ignored and Standing Bear and his people were held under military arrest by the troops of General George Crook.

General Crook did not, however, concur with the vast majority of military men who shared General Philip Sheridan's belief that "the only good Indian is a dead Indian." Crook apparently had some geniune feeling for the suffering of the Indians and a disgust for the stupidity of the government's Indian policy.

Confronted with the onerous job of herding thirty Poncas back to the land of death, he went to see a newsman in Omaha who also sympathized with the Indians. In fact these two men were reportedly the only whites ever to have been initiated into the exclusive Sioux Soldier Lodge.

There now entered into Bright Eyes' life one of the most remarkable men of the Western frontier. Omaha newsman Thomas Tibbles had already had a colorful career up to this point and much was ahead of him. As a young boy he had run away from home to live with the Sioux. Next he had joined up with John Brown in the Missouri-Kansas border wars and was nearly lynched by the notorious terrorist Quantrell. Following service in the Civil War, Tibbles became a gun-toting frontier minister, standing off ill-tempered toughs who didn't take kindly to churches. He next began a tumultuous career as a frontier newspaperman. Among the causes he had already championed when Crook approached him was relief for the Nebraska farmers who had been wiped out by hordes of grasshoppers and whose starving condition had been suppressed from public attention by land speculators. Tibbles, a giant for that time at six foot four inches, was an experienced and knowledgeable fighter whether with gun or a typecase.

Now Crook wanted Tibbles to help in another situation of injustice and hardship. As Tibbles wrote years later, Crook told him that he must "go into this fight against those who are robbing these helpless people. You can win; I'm sure of it. The American people, if they knew half the truth, would send every member of the Indian Ring to prison."

Tibbles not only set about publicizing the Poncas' situation immediately but enlisted the aid of a prominent attorney. The two began an effort to obtain a writ of habeus corpus to secure the release of Standing Bear and the other Poncas held by Crook's men. Bright Eyes soon joined their effort, providing Tibbles with a written account of the Poncas' case. Her document was the principle one upon which was built the historic court case that was to ensue and her handwritten manuscript still survives from 1879.

Bright Eyes and her brother Frank secured the permission of the Indian agent to go to Omaha for the critical court hearing. It was there that she first met Tibbles and the church people he had enlisted to support the case.

On the morning of April 30, 1879, the court convened to hear argument on the request for a writ.

Tibbles and the attorney had decided to base their argument on the Fourteenth Amendment which had been, as Tibbles noted, "adopted only eleven years earlier and (was) still comparatively untested."

Under the Fourteenth Amendment all persons are guaranteed due process of law and equal protection of the laws. The essential question in that pioneer Omaha courtroom was whether or not an Indian was a person under the law and thus entitled to protection of the Constitution.

It took the judge over a week to research his decision. Thirty-five years later, Tibbles wrote of that decision, ". . . I am still amazed to realize that it has been ignored by historians," for the judge had concluded that "an Indian is a person within the laws of the United States."

Under this landmark decision and as persons within the law, the thirty Poncas were free to remain with the Omahas. But for Bright Eyes and the others the fight had just begun. Although Standing Bear and his band of thirty were secure in their homeland, there yet remained the rest of the Poncas still on the Arkansas River. And beyond the immediate fate of the Poncas were still the questions of the Omahas' future and that of territorial guarantees to all Indian tribes.

What was needed was a long term effort in the courts to secure Indian rights. In order to obtain sufficient funds for such an effort, Bright Eyes, her brother Frank, Standing Bear, and Tibbles prepared to head East to campaign for funds. It was the beginning of a century-long struggle for justice for American Indians.

Initially Tibbles had doubts about Bright Eyes going on the tour. Her presence would require that of her brother as chaperone, thus adding to the expenses to be met by the church people underwriting the effort. He was also concerned about her effectiveness as a speaker. At her first appearance she was, he noted, "plainly frightened almost out of her senses, like a bird in a net, but hers was a graceful, appealing fright that never lost its dignity."

After initial speaking engagements in Omaha, the group entrained for the East. Tibbles had already established a base of personal support in Boston through his earlier abolitionist work, including among his acquaintances the influential Wendell Phillips and noted writer Edward Everett Hale. Additionally, newspaper accounts of the Poncas' plight based on stories filed by Tibbles had roused the same element in Boston that had rallied to the abolitionist cause twenty-five years earlier.

En route to their Eastern enclave of support, the fund-raising team stopped at Chicago and other major cities, and everywhere their reception was rewarding. Lecture halls and churches were packed; reception lines and dinners abounded. But Boston, the self-styled center of the universe of the 19th century, was the principle target. In Boston were the leading intellectuals and opinion-makers of the period.

The Boston campaign began well, with a reception by the mayor and the news that the group was to be guests of the city for a week. On the first day in Boston, however, personal tragedy confronted them. Telegrams arrived informing them that Tibbles' wife had died suddenly back in Nebraska and Standing Bear's brother had been shot to death by government agents in the Indian Territory.

The two men steeled themselves against their grief and that night carried the Indian cause to a large reception in their honor. But even in their grief and shock the four campaigners realized that there was ominous meaning in the shooting of Standing Bear's brother. The campaign they had begun was challenging powerful interests and now it was clear that their relatives in Nebraska and Indian Territory were virtually hostages. But the group did not falter.

The reception that night was a great success: the story of the wrongs done the Omahas and Poncas and, by extension, all Indians stirred the audience assembled in Boston's Horticultural Hall. "We are thinking men and women," Bright Eyes told the Bostonians. "Your government has no right to say to us, go here, or go there, and if we show any reluctance, to force us to do it at the point of a bayonet."

The efforts of Bright Eyes and the others ignited the support of the city activists. The mayor of Boston became treasurer of the Boston Committee formed to aid the Indians. Others who joined up included Alice Longfellow, Senator Henry Daves, Louis Brandeis, publisher H. O. Houghton and numerous clergymen, business leaders and Harvard professors. The conscience of America was for the first time confronted with the nation's crimes against the Indians.

The presence of Bright Eyes perhaps more than anything else drew the attention and interest of the intellectual leadership of the day. She was personally attractive, small and gentle, a pretty though sombre little figure as she stood onstage translating for Standing Bear or delivering her own passionate pleas for her people.

Bright Eyes insisted upon always wearing "civilized" clothes, a dark dress endlessly varied with changes of scarf or collar. But many of the literary people she encountered wanted to impose upon her that 19th century romantic and sentimental view of Indians that ironically persisted at the same time that the "noble savage" was being routinely exterminated. Bright Eyes was, for the intellectual Bostonians, an "Indian maiden" and "an Indian princess," a veritable embodiment

of the literary ideal of Minnehaha of Longfellow's poem "Hiawatha."
Consequently the city was thrilled when Longfellow himself, now an
elderly man, met the shy Bright Eyes and, as tradition has it, took her
hands in his and said, "This is Minnehaha!"

Bright Eyes and her companions addressed a huge throng in
Boston's Music Hall. The crowd not only filled America's largest
auditorium but spilled over into the streets. Similar mass meetings
followed: five hundred Boston businessmen in the Merchants Hall, a
large gathering presided over by the Governor, a concert by the black
Jubilee Singers of Fiske University. And for Bright Eyes the special
honor of being the first woman to speak in historic Fanueil Hall.

At the end of the sensational month in Boston the group moved from
one Eastern city to the next, working their way to the next important
target—Washington, D.C.

The success of the Boston tour was not lost on the opponents of
Indian Rights. Those who had been exploiting the Indians for years
without interference made Bright Eyes and her companions the targets
of scurrilous attack. Men who had made fortunes selling supplies
intended for starving Indians now accused Tibbles of pocketing the
proceeds of the fund-raising campaign.

An old campaigner like Tibbles had anticipated such charges and
arranged to have all funds held by the citizen committees supporting
the cause. He was accustomed to being in the storm's eye of controversy but the experience was painful to the shy Bright Eyes.

In the midst of the worst attacks, the group gained the support of one
who was to be their most effective ally. Helen Hunt Jackson, then a
free-lance writer of little note, was drawn by both the justice of Bright
Eyes' cause and by the personality of the woman herself. From her
association with Bright Eyes, the writer was inspired to her life's work.

Immediately she began to publish attacks on the policies of the
"Indian Ring" in Washington. Ceaselessly she pounded away in
column after column in the *New York Herald*, detailing with hard facts
and thorough research the long infamy against the Indians. The work
thus begun culminated in her book *Century of Dishonor* and in later
years in the even more effective novel *Ramona*.

By the time that the entourage arrived in Washington, Helen Hunt
Jackson's columns and the outcry from other articulate champions of
the cause had softened officialdom and the stage was set. A special
Senate investigating committee convened and Bright Eyes and Standing Bear were called as witnesses. Ranged against them were the

Secretary of the Interior and other officials who held life and death powers over the Indians.

In the months that followed Bright Eyes endured the strain of simultaneously testifying before Congress and carrying on with the lecture tour. In spite of the inhuman schedule both she and Standing Bear were compelling witnesses. The Senate Committee reported in favor of the Poncas and against the Department of Interior policy that had displaced them. During this period, too, Bright Eyes was received by President Hayes.

In 1881 a bill was passed and signed into law, providing restitution to the Poncas for damages incurred in their removal and for land to be held in severalty by members of the tribe in either their old homeland or in Indian Territory. It was a significant gain but marred by a major concession to the Department of Interior. The law was interpreted to mean that the Poncas' present location represented their place of choice. Thus Standing Bear's remnant band was safe in their northern home, but the majority of the tribe was still trapped in Indian Territory.

During the year following passage of the bill concerning the Poncas, a law was passed securing in perpetuity the rights of the Omahas to their tribal lands. Bright Eyes' efforts on behalf of her people had succeeded.

At about this same time the widowed Tibbles proposed marriage to Bright Eyes and she accepted him. They were wed on July 23, 1881, in the mission church on the Omaha reservation.

It is difficult to imagine a more unlikely pair than the extroverted, towering Tibbles and the shy, diminutive Bright Eyes. Although they had worked well together as a campaign team, the underlying differences in personality and outlook would mar their relationship over the coming years. Basically Tibbles was a warhorse, ever eager to respond to the challenge of a fight on behalf of those being mistreated. Bright Eyes on the other hand, had overriden her innate shyness to enter public life for a specific purpose and when that purpose was achieved she wished to withdraw to more private efforts in furthering the welfare of her people. They remained her one true cause, while Tibbles pursued a broad range of issues.

For a time they were able to work together to some extent. Tibbles wrote a book entitled, with his usual dramatic flair, *Ploughed Under, the Story of an Indian Chief,* and Bright Eyes wrote the introduction. She was doing other writing as well, including a short story on the nature of Indian life for a leading children's magazine. She also presented a paper before the national Association of Women entitled "The Position, Occupation, and Culture of Indian Women." She and Tibbles then toured England and on their return Bright Eyes illustrated a book on the Omahas called *Oo-Ma-Ha-Ta-Wa-Tha*. Issued in 1878, it contained what was probably the first published artwork by an American Indian.

Bright Eyes and Tibbles shared one last significant experience before their interests began to seriously diverge. In 1890 they were present near the Battle of Wounded Knee. Tibbles was the first newsman to transmit an account of the tragic slaughter of the Indians, while Bright Eyes nursed the cruelly wounded Indian women and children.

The slaughter at Wounded Knee marked the end of the Indian wars and, predictably, the end of the first concerted drive for the reform of Indian affairs.

Tibbles consequently turned to a new interest, allying himself with the Populist movement on behalf of the white plains farmers. He threw himself into the political battle with his usual energy and in 1904, though the high point of Populism had passed, Thomas Tibbles was nominated candidate for Vice-President of the United States on the Populist ticket.

Bright Eyes did not live to see Tibbles' nomination. After the Battle of Wounded Knee she worked with him as a news correspondent in Washington for a Populist journal. Then they tried farming her allotment of land within the Omaha tribal lands. She was not happy unless with her people; he was not happy away from the battlefields. Once more they went Tibbles' way and returned to Washington, but in 1902, Bright Eyes' health failing, they returned to the land of the Omahas. There she died in the same year. She was only forty-nine years old at the time of her death.

Bright Eyes achieved many firsts for herself and for her people. She was the first Indian woman to become politically active, the first to be honored with a speech upon the floor of the United States Senate, the first to see her artwork in print. She helped begin a crusade for justice that yet continues. Further, she helped break the way for others in her family. Her brother Frank made important contributions to anthropology of the American Indian; all of her sisters followed her in getting an advanced education; one sister became the first woman Indian doctor while another achieved a position of leadership among the Omahas, a rare attainment for a woman among Indian tribes.

Like many women on the Western frontier, Bright Eyes paid a high price for participating in the changes that characterized the era. What it cost her in psychic wholeness to cross from one culture to the other can only be surmised.

9

Women on the Cattle Frontier

Agnes Morley Cleaveland, Pamela Mann, Ella "Cattle Kate" Watson, Elizabeth Taylor

A six-shooter makes men and women equal
Agnes Morley

In the decades following the Civil War cattle raising became big business on the Western frontier. Although cattle ranching is usually portrayed in movies and television as a completely male world dominated by gun-slinging cowboys and outlaws, the cattle culture had its share of women. A number of women were wives of ranchers and worked side by side with them in keeping books, managing the feeding of cowboy employees, and caring for stock. A number of women actually owned cattle ranches themselves.

Some had inherited them on the death of their husbands and, like Henrietta King of the mammoth King Ranch of Texas, acquired capable managers to oversee operations. Other women, like Mary Meagher of Washington Territory, managed their ranches directly. A few, like Mrs. Bishop Hiff Warren of Colorado, who ran her assets up to ten million dollars, were highly successful in what was a very volatile business.

In 1886 a young girl named Agnes Morley came to a New Mexico cattle ranch high in the Datil Mountains along with her mother, stepfather, brother Ray, and sister Lora. Agnes later wrote:

> Cattle-raising on a grand scale was the Great Adventure of the hour. Railroading had become a matter for experts, but anybody with sufficient cash could become a big rancher. My imaginative mother had about as much fitness for the role of cattle queen as could be expected from a young woman who had always leaned upon some "natural protector," but she had had her years of training in pioneer uncertainties, so she followed the new husband as confidently as she had her first.

Agnes' new stepfather had persuaded his wife to buy the big Datil ranch with the money her deceased husband had left her, but no sooner had the family built a house than the stepfather deserted and left Agnes' mother and the three young children to shift for themselves. The story of the Morleys' struggle to hang on to their ranch is not one of the great financial success stories of women in the cattle industry, but it was a story of determination, adaptability, and humor. From her experiences growing up in this situation, Agnes Morley later wrote a book called *No Life For a Lady* that has become a classic of the West and is recognized as one of the few authentic accounts of the early cow culture.

While some women developed an aptitude for ranch management, Agnes' mother was plucky but inept:

> Faced with the supervision of a well-stocked cattle range of a good many thousand acres, she rode and did her indomitable best to keep herself informed about what was happening to her livestock; but she was unable successfully to cope with the cattle-rustlers who abounded and with the proclivities of open-range cattle to wander. . . . That she survived the years that followed speaks volumes for her courage, her stamina, and her self-sacrifice. It would have been so very easy to sink under the all but overwhelming flood of hardships and disappointments that were hers.

Agnes and her brother Ray, though still in their sub-teens, took hold where their mother could not. They became expert riders, learned the stock, worked at herding, and even succeeded in retrieving some of their cattle from rustlers by the simple method of stealing them back.

By age fourteen Agnes recognized that running a cattle ranch meant more than herding cattle. Realizing that it was a business, she decided that she would learn how to keep the ranch's books. Her intentions were thwarted, however, by her mother's repeatedly sending her off to boarding school in Philadelphia. By the time Agnes had the skill and opportunity to do the books, "not even a Philadelphia lawyer, much less a Philadelphia schoolgirl, could have found much head or tail to them. But we managed 'somehow.' "

The insistence of Agnes' mother that her children get a good education came from the fact that she herself was well-educated and cultured. Although the ranch was chronically short of money, she never failed to find funds to keep the children's schooling going. Later Agnes would appreciate her mother's efforts, but at the time she felt that courses such as Rudimentary Latin had little relevancy to her life on a New Mexico cattle ranch and she resented anything that kept her away from the life she loved.

On the ranch life was real and exciting. Having immersed herself since childhood in the actual cattle operations, Agnes never felt the loneliness that her mother and many ranch women experienced. Partly to assuage this loneliness and partly to stay in touch with the outside world, Agnes' mother devoted much of her time to writing letters concerning woman suffrage and other causes. Agnes' brother Ray couldn't understand his mother using her time this way: "He screwed up his face in genuine distress. 'Mother writes too darn many letters . . . What does Susan B. Anthony know about the cow business?' "

With their mother absorbed in her letter writing campaigns and the children periodically away at school, the cattle ranch limped along in ragged fashion. Bankruptcy threatened several times, and on one occasion went as far as the stock being rounded up for sale at sheriff's auction. Agnes was desolate but took some comfort from the assurance that her favorite horse would not be sold. Then she found out that the horse, Gray Dick, had been taken by the sheriff's deputy, "a man I had never liked because of his cruelty to horses."

Agnes set out to get her horse back. "Subsequent happenings," she said, "made local history." She pursued the deputy sheriff and overtook him as he stood talking with a group of cowhands who were helping him move the ranch's stock. When the deputy refused to return her horse, Agnes galloped toward Gray Dick, plunging right through the herd of horses and scattering them in every direction. Her reins got away from her, her horse tripped, she flew into the air and came down in a somersault. Instantly she was on her feet and unhobbling Gray Dick.

When the deputy tried to interfere, Agnes picked up a strap weighted with a heavy bell, and warned him off. "One step closer and I'll brain you with this bell." The deputy backed away and Agnes got her horse.

Later a cowhand told her that several of the men had watched the proceedings with their hands on their guns, "waitin' to see if you missed your shot with that bell, but o' course we didn't want to spoil your play."

The cowboys' restraint in letting Agnes handle her own situation was indicative of a basic willingness in the West to let people, whether women or not, do what they thought they could. In a land where competence and self-reliance meant survival, women had the opportunity to develop beyond what they were allowed to in more settled areas.

Yet there remained among cowmen a basic chivalry toward women that became legendary. Even among outlaws respect for women was strong. Agnes experienced this when she was on the trail alone and met a horseman in the dark. The rider passed her with a soft-spoken, "Good evening, Miss." Within an hour the man, who was on the run from the law, was dead. Rather than take her fresh horse and insure his getaway, he had stopped some way beyond and tried to steal a fresh mount. He was overtaken in the corral and shot by the sheriff. "He threw away his chance, and his life with it, to protect a young girl from a bad fright."

Although chivalry was strong and usually reliable, some women began to rely on it less in insuring their safety. A fair number, Agnes among them, began to carry guns. Once when she was again out alone on the trail she met a horseman, this time a Mexican who was shocked at her being alone, since Mexican women were never allowed such freedom of movement. When he expressed concern for her safety, Agnes pulled out her "little thirty-two." The Mexican said, "Bueno!" and rode off, reassured that this young girl could take care of herself.

"A six-shooter does give one a sense of security," Agnes reflected. "We had a saying, 'A six-shooter makes all men equal.' I amended it to 'A six-shooter makes men and women equal.' "

Armed women in the West are usually portrayed as being bandits or the consorts of bandits—women such as Belle Starr or Cattle Annie. But the adoption of the gun by ordinary women as an equalizer in relationships with the opposite sex was a much more radical step and a more significant one. It was indicative of how the conditions of the frontier forced women to expand their image of themselves beyond that of the passive and helpless female.

Agnes was never forced to use her "equalizer." Several occasions arose when she was in a tight spot, but each time she used her wits instead of her gun. In one situation two suspicious horsemen rode up to the ranch house at nightfall and Agnes demonstrated more coolness and self-confidence than would have been required to pull a trigger. She asked the men in and got them into an all-night poker game. Playing well enough to stay always a little ahead of them and thus keep their interest solely in the game, she whooped and hollered and generated all the fun that was expected in the cowboy's favorite past-time.

> We groaned dismally, or exulted loudly, over losses and gains; we called one another names and made dire bodily threats upon one another. 'Gimme two, and watch me cut Miss Agnes' throat and get

back my pile she done stole from me' — 'Draw to your hand girl, draw to your hand; think I'll fall for that blazer?' — 'Now, Mr. Red' (the only name I knew him by), 'here's where you land in your narrow grave, just six by three, and the wild coyotes will howl with glee.'

The all-night poker game ended up with the strangers making breakfast and doing the dishes while Agnes came out twenty cents ahead. Later she found out that her suspicions concerning the pair had been correct; they were "bad hombres" on the run.

The self-reliance that women on cattle ranches developed was a necessity even among those who were married, since men were commonly gone on long cattle drives or buying trips. The entire operation of the cattle industry would not have been possible without the ability of women to endure the long absences of their men in an area where the next nearest ranch might be thirty miles away. "It was this deadly staying at home month after month," wrote Agnes of those women who had husbands, "keeping a place of refuge ready for their men when they returned from their farings-forth that called for the greater courage, I think. Men walked in a sort of perpetual adventure, but women waited . . ."

In this respect Agnes had no doubts that she and her mother and sister were luckier than the women who had a man to run the place. "Not many of our women neighbors got about as did my mother and her daughters. Not many had reason to, with their menfolks to carry the responsibility of looking after their cattle."

She rejoiced in her ability to take care of herself and the resulting freedom it brought and in the skills she had acquired in ranching. But her development beyond the stereotype of "lady" was by no means an even process.

Like most women of the time, she rode sidesaddle and continued to do so for ten years, though later it was a "mystery" to her that she had done so. Before she could give up the sidesaddle, however, she had to work through the matter of proper clothing:

> First, I discarded, or rather refused to adopt, the sunbonnet, conventional headgear of my female neighbors. When I went unashamedly about under a five-gallon (not ten-gallon) Stetson, many an eyebrow was raised; then followed a double-breasted blue flannel shirt, with white pearl buttons, frankly unfeminine. In time came blue denim knickers worn under a short blue denim skirt. Slow evolution (or was it decadence?) toward a costume suited for immediate needs. Decadence having set in, the descent from the existing standards of female modesty to purely human comfort and convenience was swift. A man's saddle

and a divided skirt (awful monstrosity that was) were inevitable. This was in the middle nineties.

Liberation in terms of clothing and in riding astride meant that Western women were moving toward a new attitude regarding their bodies. In the face of the frailty and delicacy that were part of the ideal of femininity in that period, women like Agnes were learning to be proud of their physical competence and skills. After watching Agnes control a difficult horse, a scout from Buffalo Bill's Wild West show made her an offer to join the troupe. Agnes had no desire to ride broncos for money; her pride lay in the fact that she could keep a horse *from* bucking.

In the mid-1890's both Agnes and her brother were sent away to college, she to Stanford University and he to Columbia. There then developed what Agnes called "our Jekyll-Hyde lives." Ray was no longer solely a New Mexico cowman; he was also a New York college man and one of the country's earliest football heroes. Agnes had a similar problem sorting out her identity as she went back and forth between the California campus and the New Mexico cattle ranch.

On one occasion she took a sorority sister home with her:

> In time she confessed that before she left for Datil "the sisters in the bonds" had taken her aside and said to her: "Grace, we want you to take careful note while you are visiting Agnes. You know, Agnes worries us. She seems to be a truthful enough person generally, but we just can't believe all the things she tells us about that New Mexico cattle ranch. Just keep your eyes open and report."
>
> Three weeks on the ranch—and Grace wrote the sisterhood "I want to report that Agnes' stories indicate admirable self-restraint on her part."

Ray wavered between becoming a civil engineer and continuing with ranching, finally choosing to stay with cattle. In 1899 Agnes married a mining student she met on the Stanford campus, and "schism between my own opposed lives was made permanent." The couple settled in California but for Agnes "New Mexico always remained home."

Agnes' sense of a Jekyll-Hyde aspect to her life was well-founded. Women on the cattle frontier straddled a dual existence. They were at one and the same time the objects of chivalrous deference on the part of men (such treatment even being accorded prostitutes) so prized were women because of their scarceness on the frontier. But at the same time that they were accorded chivalry, women were able to enjoy a degree of independence and scope for expression of their abilities. One authority on the West, Lewis Atherton, has noted "Except possibly for those who stemmed from the Old South plantation tradition, ranchers liked women of an independent turn of mind and faith in their ability to take care of themselves."

The "code of the West," dictating that all women be treated gently, as "ladies," could be stretched therefore to allow women to be strong, assertive, and competent. It is likely that men on the cattle frontier, engaged as they were in so much activity that clearly demonstrated their masculinity, felt less challenged by strong women than did their Eastern counterparts.

"Grit" in a woman was admired not only in the form of persistence and courage but even when it took such extreme form as the defiance that Pamela Mann of Texas displayed toward Sam Houston during the Texas-Mexican War. As the Texan civilians and soldiers fled the Mexicans over the muddy roads to Nacogdoches in 1836, Houston's army commandeered a yoke of oxen from Pamela Mann to pull the heavy cannon over the muddy trail. It was her understanding that the oxen were to be used only so long as the army kept toward Nacogdoches. When the army turned toward Harrisburg, Pamela Mann went after her oxen, taking with her a pair of pistols and a long knife.

She overtook Houston after about ten miles. "The woman defied the whole army. She rode up to the General and addressed him: 'General, you told me a damn lie, you said that you was going on the Nacogdoches road. Sir, I want my oxen.' Houston replied that the cannon could not be moved without them. Her rejoinder came ripping back: 'I don't care a damn for your cannon, I want my oxen.''

She held a gun on Houston, jumped down from her horse, and cut her oxen loose with the long knife she had brought. "Nobody said a word," a witness noted in his diary. "She jumpt on her horse with whip in hand, and way she went in a lope with her oxen." The incident was ever after known in Texas annals as "Houston's Defeat." "Such hardihood could never have been developed within the tradition-bound borders of the eastern states," one historian wrote of her. "The early Texans had a healthy respect for this woman who blazed her own very characteristic trail on the frontier."

The tolerance of men on the cattle frontier for defiance in women had its limits, however. If there was one thing more sacred to a cattleman than women, it was his cattle. The code of the West was lenient on women but very rough on rustlers or anyone who interfered with the practices of the open range. Two women who were believed to have overstepped the line in these respects were lynched, one in Wyoming and one in Nebraska.

The first and more famous of these two women was Ella Watson, afterwards known as "Cattle Kate." Ella had a small ranch near the Sweetwater River in Wyoming not far from the road ranch of her friend, saloon-storekeeper Jim Averell. Both properties were in the middle of a huge tract of grazing land claimed by one of the area's biggest cattlemen who was an important member of the powerful Wyoming Stock Growers' Association. Threatened by the intrusion of small cattle ranchers and farmers, the big cattlemen were intent on frightening small stockmen and "nesters" out of the area.

They chose to make an example of Averell apparently because of his open criticism of the organization's members and methods. In Ella's case, though there was actually no evidence of her being a rustler, they were highly suspicious of the rate at which she acquired cattle. On July 20, 1888, a party of stockmen rode up to Ella's house. A fourteen-year-old boy was there and saw what happened:

> I was at Ella's trying to catch a pony. John Durbin took down the wire fence and drove the cattle out, while McLain and Conners kept Ella from going to the house. After a while they told her to get into the wagon and she asked them where they were going. They told her to Rawlins. She wanted to go into the house and change her clothes but they would not let her and made her get into the wagon. Bothwell told her he would rope her and drag her if she did not get in.

The party then drove on to Averell's place, brushing aside the young boy's attempt to interfere. After they picked up Averell the men took the two to Spring Creek where, one of the party later testified, they had originally intended to dunk the pair and thereby scare them into leaving the area. There was, however, little water in the river and the party moved on. At a place about five miles from Averell's ranch, they halted. Here they were overtaken by a cowboy who had been alerted by the young boy and had ridden after the lynch party, armed only with a six-shooter against six rifles.

"Bothwell had the rope around Jim's neck and had it tied to a limb," cowboy Frank Buchanan stated afterwards. "He told him to be game and jump off (the wagon). McLain was trying to put the rope around Ella's neck, but she was dodging her head so that he did not succeed at that time. I opened fire on them but do not know whether I hit anyone or not. They turned and began shooting at me. I unloaded my revolver twice but had to run as they were shooting at me with

Winchesters. I ran to my horse and rode to the ranch and told them Jim and Ella were hung.''

No sooner was Ella Watson dead than the stockmen started a press campaign in which she was transformed into "Cattle Kate," characterized as having not only rustled more cattle than any man in the West but as having been a prostitute, husband-poisoner, and hold-up artist. So effective was the smear campaign that young Owen Wister, later the author of *The Virginian,* was among those taken in, recording in his diary: "Sat yesterday in smoking car with one of the gentlemen indicted for lynching the man and woman. He seemed a good solid citizen and I hope he'll get off.''

None of the participants in the lynching were convicted, although they had been identified by several witnesses. Instead the witnesses disappeared or died one by one, among them the courageous cowboy Frank Buchanan and the fourteen-year-old boy.

The lynching was one of the opening skirmishes in Wyoming's notorious Johnson County War between the stockholders association and the rest of the citizenry. The stockgrowers won this skirmish but there were bigger battles ahead that they would lose. The lynching of Ella Watson remained, however, what one historian has termed "the most revolting crime in the entire annals of the west.''

Hardly less infamous was the hanging of Elizabeth Taylor in Nebraska three years earlier. The Taylor case also involved matters of wandering cattle and property questions. Elizabeth and her brother, who had joined her in running her ranch after her husband's death, were defiant and persistent in quarrels with their neighbors over wandering stock. Steadily their neighbors' resentment mounted.

The climax came when one of the neighbors was shot dead near the Taylor spread, most likely by a drifter cowboy from Texas who had been working for Elizabeth. The Texan disappeared immediately and friends of the dead man along with enemies of Elizabeth moved to fasten the murder on her. When official justice could not be pushed against her fast enough to suit her enemies, a mob took Elizabeth and her brother and hung them both.

Like Ella Watson, without substantiation Elizabeth Taylor was subsequently accused of having poisoned her deceased husband and also of having paid off her ranch hands by "entertaining" them. The technique of painting a woman as husband-killer and whore seemed to be a necessary ingredient in salving the image if not the conscience of men who committed the crime of lynching a woman.

In time the violence of the Western cattle lands ebbed away. By the

1890's when Agnes Morley was carrying a gun, she admitted that range people were going armed long after weapons were needed for more than shooting rattlesnakes. Steadily, guns were set aside by both men and women as the pioneer era closed.

Something remained, however, of the hardiness and self-confidence that women had gained by holding their own in a violent era. When women originally had come to the cattle frontier they rode sidesaddle, if at all; by the close of the pioneer cattle era women not only rode astride but with such expertise and daring that some of the best of them became rodeo champions and stars of the wild West shows.

Sarah J. Lippincott, who wrote of her travels in the West under the pen name of "Grace Greenwood," encountered some of the earliest predecessors of women rodeo riders. The first of these she saw in Denver in 1871 at a Saturday night circus. "I had unmixed delight in the wonderful riding, skill and daring, quiet confidence and matchless physical strength, of a young California girl, called Polly Lee. She managed, with the utmost ease and grace, four horses, having four younger brothers and sisters swarming all over her. She supports, in more ways than one, the whole family."

Although Sarah was shocked by the "horrible undress" of two women tumblers in a prior act at the circus, her remarks about these acrobats applied as well to the women who had left behind Victorian frailty and delicacy and become frontier horsewomen: "it was something to see that women could be so courageous, so skillful, and so strong—could attain such steadiness of nerve and firmness of muscle."

Months later at a county fair, the writer had progressed in her ideas about suitable clothing for active women. "There was the usual display of lady equestrianism; a good deal of solemn cantering around the track . . . and all was very proper and commonplace, except the performances of a certain young lady, who rode a bare-back act on a spirited white horse which she sat with the utmost ease and dignity and managed admirably." When her favorite did not win a prize, Sarah was angry. "I should have like to set those judges . . . each on a bare-backed, high-mettled steed, and I would have compelled them to ride sidewise and encumbered with a long, heavy skirt . . . I think their respect for such performances would have increased."

A year after Sarah Lippincott applauded the bare-back rider, Cheyenne, Wyoming, held what was probably the first real rodeo. Almost thirty years were to pass, however, before women were allowed in competition. Again Cheyenne led the way, this time admitting Bertha Kaepernick as the first woman rodeo competitor. She was followed into rodeo by an increasing number of women over the years, possibly the first professional competitive women athletes in America.

Over the decades women came a long way on the cattle frontier. Looking back over her life in New Mexico, Agnes Morley recalled the first time she confronted the question of woman's place on the ranching frontier. Her brother Ray had announced one day while they were still children, "Y' know, cow business is man's business. Women oughten to be doin' it."

Agnes' reply was one that many women from Texas to Montana could join in: "Is *that* so?"

Anna Howard Shaw *Photograph Courtesy of Sophia Smith Collection*

Professional Women in the West

Anna Howard Shaw and Bethenia Owens-Adair

It is better she should die doing the thing she wants to do than she should die
because she can't do it

*Mary A.Livermore's
advice to Anna Howard Shaw*

Writing of her life in pioneer Michigan in the 1850's and 60's, Anna Howard Shaw described a condition that pretty well prevailed on America's frontier throughout history. Cash was chronically short on most of the Western frontier, and jobs of any kind for women or men were often scarce.

> The largest salary I could earn by teaching in our Northern woods was one hundred and fifty-six dollars a year, for two terms of thirteen weeks each; and from this, of course, I had to deduct the cost of my board and clothing—the sole expenditure I allowed myself. The dollars for an education accumulated very, very slowly, until at last, in desperation, weary of seeing the years of my youth rush past, bearing my hopes with them, I took a sudden and radical step. I gave up teaching, left our cabin in the woods, and went to Big Rapids . . . There, I had decided, I would learn a trade of some kind, of any kind. The sole essential was that it should be a money-making trade, offering wages which would make it possible to add more rapidly to my savings. In those days . . . in a small pioneer town, the fields open to women were few and unfruitful. The needle at once presented itself, but at first I turned with loathing from it. I would have preferred the digging of ditches or the shoveling of coal; but the needle alone persistently pointed out my way, and I was finally forced to take it.

One notable exception, of course, was the Western mining camp where money in the form of gold dust was more plentiful and the demand for the services of women—scarce as women were—was very high. In her letters from the California goldmines, Dame Shirley described one woman who had earned "nine hundred dollars in nine weeks, clear of all expenses, by washing." Some women opened boarding houses and made more money providing food and bed than did their husbands mining gold. Other women opened another kind of house, offering bed alone to the womanless miners and later the cowboys and other males of the Western frontier.

But the women of the West who sought to earn their own way were not all washerwomen, landladies, or prostitutes. Some number, like Anna Shaw and. Bethenia Owens-Adair, aspired to more challenging positions in life. They sought to enter the professions at a time when women, both East and West, were pioneering against the firm prejudice that woman's place was absolutely by the hearth.

On balance it is difficult to judge who had the hardest time breaking the barriers that were firmly implanted against careers for women. In the East conventions were stronger, but schooling was more available. In the West prejudice may have been less since recognition of the individual's responsibility for his or her survival was strong, but in the West advanced education was difficult to obtain in the early decades and the problem of supporting oneself while going to school was considerable. As late as the 1890's in Nebraska, writer Willa Cather for example seriously overworked herself while trying to keep both college studies and her newspaper writing going.

For women like Anna Howard Shaw and Bethenia Owens-Adair, pioneer women in the ministry and medicine, the battle was incredibly difficult. In many ways the experiences of these two women and others like them on the frontier were more harrowing than those of the pioneer wives and mothers who held off Indian raids with the family rifle or endured the sacrifices and suffering of the overland trail. The career of wife and mother on the Western frontier was certainly a full-time one and a deeply gratifying one—families would literally perish without the work of a capable and skilled woman—but at least the pioneer wife and mother had the support and approval of society in her job. The women who sought to work in the professions, on the other hand, walked a hard and lonely road, often as virtual outcasts.

Yet if the Western frontier offered severe obstacles against obtaining an education and a career, the frontier experience itself seems to have built into its women a hardihood, determination, and a sense of confidence that were less common in the gentler Eastern society where women of the upper classes were kept as petted, mindless darlings while lower class women were consigned to the grim and underpaid work of mills and sweat shops.

As a child on the frontier, Anna not only developed the stamina for what lay ahead but gained a strong feeling that she had *earned* the right to make of her life what she would. At the age of twelve she along with her mother, her young sisters Mary and Eleanor, and her eight-year-old brother Harry were suddenly confronted with surviving solely by their own efforts in the primitive isolation of the Michigan wilderness. They had been sent to the northern woods by Anna's father who was supposed to follow them immediately into their new home. An older brother, age eighteen, came with them originally but was taken ill almost immediately and returned east. Of their arrival at their frontier home, Anna later wrote:

> My mother's mental picture was, naturally, of an English farm. Possibly she had visions of red barns and deep meadows, sunny skies and daisies. What we found awaiting us were the four walls and the roof of a good-sized log-house, standing in a small cleared strip of the wilderness, its doors and windows represented by square holes, its floor also a thing of the future, its whole effect achingly forlorn and desolate . . . I shall never forget the look my mother turned upon the place . . . She could not realize even then, I think, that this was really the place father had prepared for us, that here he expected us to live. When she finally took it in she buried her face in her hands and in that way she sat for hours without moving or speaking. For the first time in her life she had forgotten us; and we, for our part, dared not speak to her. . . . Our little world had crumbled under our feet. Never before had we seen our mother give way to despair.

Anna's mother rallied somewhat and in time was doing the tasks necessary to clothe the family. Anna's father, on the other hand, proved a complete failure at providing for his family. For eighteen long months he did not join them and when he did arrive he turned out to be of no use on a frontier farm, preferring to spend his energies in planning, philosophizing, and concocting dreams of success.

Faced with starvation the young children stepped into adult roles almost overnight. Mary and Eleanor took on all the indoor work of food preparation while twelve-year-old Anna and eight-year-old Harry teamed up to take care of all outdoor work. No land had been cleared for planting so the two youngsters immediately set about grubbing up the sod without the aid of a plow in order to plant what they could. The crops were meager the first two seasons, but the two children were greatly encouraged by the results of their efforts.

In addition to getting in the life-saving crops, Anna and Harry laid a floor in the new cabin. Having calmly mastered carpentry (using wood hauled in by a neighbor), they next set about learning how to fell trees and in time became experts. They also gathered wild food, took care of livestock as it was acquired, plowed when a plow was obtained, made furniture, and did all the other heavy labor of a frontier farm.

Their most remarkable undertaking was the digging of the well. Weary after a year of hauling water or melting snow in winter, they cut themselves a forked stick and water-witched the most likely location for a well. The two youngsters then proceeded not only to dig the well but to line its sides in a most satisfactory manner. Their work was so good that the well served the family without problems for the entire twelve years they remained on the farm.

One of the jobs undertaken by the pair was more fun than work, and that was fishing. They devised their own unorthodox system for catching fish in the neighboring river utilizing, symbolically enough, wire from a discarded hoop-skirt.

The work thus toughened the children both physically and mentally. They quickly learned that they could figure out a way to meet almost any situation. "Naturally," Anna wrote matter of factly, "our greatest menaces were wild animals and Indians (but) . . . we grew indifferent." On several occasions, however, this indifference was challenged. One evening as the two were going to fetch the family cow they met a party of Indians in the darkening woods. Aware that they were completely vulnerable because they were alone, Anna concluded that the only thing to do was to act completely unafraid. She and Harry went along, pretending to play with the rope brought to fetch the cow, like "care-free children." The Indians passed them by without even a glance.

When she was thirteen Anna had her first chance at schooling, rudimentary though it was. Gradually she began to think of getting a better education and then there grew in her the desire to be a minister, a dream she gave flesh to by standing on tree stump pulpits and preaching to the trees. It seemed for a long time like a hopeless dream, particularly when the Civil War took the men, including the now older Harry, away from the farm and even more work fell to Anna who was, by this time, teaching as well as farming. But then things changed:

> The end of the Civil War brought freedom to me too. When peace was declared my father and brothers returned to the claim in the wilderness which we women of the family had labored so desperately to hold while they were gone . . . After the return of our men it was no longer necessary to devote every penny of my earnings to the maintenance of our home. For the first time I could begin to save a portion of my

income toward the fulfillment of my college dream, but even yet there was a long arid stretch ahead of me before the college doors came even distantly into sight.

It was then that Anna moved to the village of Big Rapids and undertook to earn her way with the hated needlework. She was at last taking a step toward her dream, but needlework paid little more than teaching.

"Fate, however, as if weary at last of seeing me between her paws, suddenly let me escape." A woman minister came to Big Rapids and not only rekindled Anna's ambition but gave her good advice. ". . . as I listened to her sermon, thrilled to the soul, all my early aspiration to become a minister myself stirred in me with cumulative force." Anna confided her dream to the woman minister who told her, "My child, give up your foolish idea of learning a trade and go to school. You can't do anything until you have an education. Get it, and get it *now*."

Anna immediately stopped sewing and enrolled in the Big Rapids High School, which she proudly noted "was also a preparatory school for college." For once she let her family take care of her, accepting room and board with her married sister. Other needs were taken in stride: ". . . the wardrobe I had brought from the woods covered me sufficiently; to one who had walked five and six miles a day for years, walking to school held no discomfort, and as for pleasure, I found it, like a heroine of fiction, in my studies. For the first time life was smiling at me, and with all my young heart I smiled back."

A sympathetic teacher, aware of Anna's ministerial ambitions, guided her into classes on public speaking and "elocution." The first time she faced an audience, however, she fainted from nervousness. Gallantly she picked herself up from the floor and started over again from the beginning. Although she was painfully embarrassed she felt that "if I let that failure stand against me I could never more afterward speak in public." In what was the equivalent of getting back on the horse that had thrown her, Anna conquered fear. Thereafter in her long career addressing congregations, lecture audiences, and women's suffrage rallies, she was one of the most confident speakers to ever mount a pulpit or platform.

Yet between her and these attainments lay much greater problems than the stagefright she had overcome before her first audience. As Anna progressed in high school and tried to earn money for college, her desire to become a minister raised a considerable amount of opposition among her friends. One of these friends pleaded with a visiting lecturer to dissuade Anna from the course she had set herself, arguing that the effort was wearing her down and would surely kill her. The lecturer, Mary A. Livermore, then at the height of her own career, first addressed her reply to Anna: "If you want to preach, go on and preach. Don't let anybody stop you. No matter what people say, don't let them stop you." And then to Anna's friend she said. "It is better that she should die doing the thing she wants to than that she should die because she can't do it."

The opposition from Anna's family to her proposed career was vehement. When she was invited by a minister to give a sermon, the family was so scandalized by what they believed to be a disgrace that they took out an advertisement in the local newspaper:

> *A young girl named Anna Shaw, seventeen years old, preached at Ashton yesterday. Her real friends deprecate the course she is pursuing.*

There was to be plenty of deprecation—from male classmates in theology courses at an Eastern seminary, from officials in the Methodist Church when she sought ordination, from the "tough" males in her first congregation on Cape Cod. But she stuck to her course through it all and became a fully-ordained minister. She had wanted to preach and she did. After one of her sermons, a man who had strongly opposed her said to her landlady, "Her sermon? Huh! I don't know what she preached. But say, don't make no mistake about one thing: the little preacher has sure got grit."

In 1885 she added a medical degree to her doctorate in divinity, completing studies that year at Boston Medical School. She had taken the degree without intending to practice medicine but for the purpose of adding a new dimension to her thinking. She carried on her medical studies while also carrying the work of two congregations. "Congenial work, no matter how much there is of it, has never killed anyone." To someone who had felled trees and dug a well at age twelve, nothing seemed too difficult.

It was perhaps inevitable that she would join the women's suffrage movement. Eventually she became one of its leaders, traveling the country in the company of Susan B. Anthony. It was this work that took her West again, everywhere from Kansas to California, lecturing and campaigning in all kinds of weather and circumstances. She recalled:

> To drive fifty or sixty miles in a day to meet a lecture engagement was a frequent experience. I have been driven across the praries in June when they were like a mammoth flower-bed, and in January when they seemed one huge snow-covered grave—my grave, I thought at times

. . . when the thermometer was twenty degrees below zero . . .

On one occasion aboard a snowbound train in Minnesota she found herself the only woman among a car full of cattlemen. One of them stopped playing cards and asked her to lecture on woman suffrage so as to help pass the time away. It was an unlikely topic for an unlikely audience.

> Their card-playing had seemed to me a sinful thing (I was stricter in my views then than I am today), and I was glad to create a diversion. . . When I had finished they seemed to think some slight return was in order, so they proceeded to make a bed for me. They took the bottoms out of two seats, arranged them crosswise, and one man folded his overcoat into a pillow. Inspired by this, two others immediately donated their fur overcoats for upper and lower coverings. When the bed was ready they waved me toward it with a most hospitable air, and I crept in between the overcoats and slumbered sweetly until I was aroused the next morning by the welcome music of a snowplow . . .

Farther west, cowmen on another occasion responded even more heartily to her suffrage speaking.

> In Oregon we were joined by Miss Lucy Anthony. There at Pendleton, I spoke during the great "round-up," holding the meeting at night on the street, in which thousands of horsemen—cowboys, Indians, and ranchmen—were riding up and down, blowing horns, shouting and singing. It seemed impossible to interest an audience under such conditions but . . . never have we had more courteous or enthusiastic listeners . . . Best of all, they not only cheered our sentiments, but they followed up with their votes . . . and when I had finished one of the cowboys rode close to me and asked for my New York address. "You will hear from me later," he said.

Not long afterward a banner arrived at the New York headquarters of the suffrage movement, sporting a pen-and-ink sketch of the cowboy and his horse over which were superimposed the words: WOMAN SUFFRAGE—WE ARE ALL FOR IT.

In the closing years of her life Anna Howard Shaw wrote a book of her experiences entitled *The Story of a Pioneer,* published in 1915. Though woman suffrage was yet in the future, she was greatly heartened by the responsiveness of the Western states in granting women the right to vote. Although this had become for her "the Great Cause," the abilities and commitment she brought to it grew out of her success in becoming a minister and thus, in turn, out of her life in the Western woods.

The frontier experiences of Bethenia Owens-Adair, though separated by half a continent from those of Anna Howard Shaw, were
strikingly similar in terms of difficulties encountered and persistence in
meeting those difficulties. Bethenia's family was among the earliest
settlers in Oregon Territory, heading west in 1843 when she was three
years old. The Owens family, which was eventually to include nine
children, settled southwest of Astoria in coastal Oregon. Like Shaw,
Bethenia spent much of her childhood doing family chores, particularly taking care of the many younger children. "I was the family
nurse, and it was seldom that I had not a child in my arms . . . Where
there is a baby every two years, there is always no end of nursing to be
done . . . ."

Bethenia's brother Flem was her "constant companion," and the
two enjoyed fighting one another to see who was the stronger. Flem,
though younger, was bigger, but he never got the best of Bethenia
during her tomboy years. The tiny Bethenia's tomboyishness seems to
have been based not only on competition with her brother but on the
general frontier admiration for strength. "My father, a tall athletic
Kentuckian, served as sheriff of Pike County for many years, beginning as a deputy at the age of sixteen. It was often said of him:
'Thomas Owens is not afraid of man or the devil.' "

Watching her father build a fine family farm on the Oregon frontier
and seeing her younger brother outpace her in growth and strength,
Bethenia admitted that, "The regret of my life up to the age of
thirty-five was that I had not been born a boy, for I realized very early
in life that a girl was hampered and hemmed in on all sides simply by
the accident of sex."

Bethenia did try, however, to follow the principle course then open
to women. At the age of fourteen, in the manner of the frontier in
marrying young, she became the wife of LeGrand Hill, a man who had
worked on her father's farm. She went to marriage with all the
womanly delight of the time in furnishing out a new home and a new
life. "I spent all my time in preparing for my approaching marriage. I
had four quilts already pieced and ready for the lining . . . (mother)
also gave me muslin for four sheets, two pairs of pillow-cases, two
tablecloths, and four towels. I cut and made two calico dresses for
myself, and assisted in the making of my wedding dress, which was a
pretty, sky-blue figured lawn."

The hopes and enthusiasm that Bethenia had for a happy traditional
marriage were soon crushed by disillusionment. When she looked up at
her husband—he was five foot eleven inches tall and she could fit

snugly under one of his arms—she must have thought that she had married the kind of man her father was—a strong, able, and responsible person who would provide for his family and take pride in doing so. Indeed, her husband was off to a far better start than her father had been when he first reached Oregon. To the marriage Bethenia had brought a goodly array of pots and pans, her father's credit in buying groceries (which she did on the afternoon following her wedding), a riding mare, two cows and a heifer, a wagon and harness and considerable furniture including "a good feather bed." Her husband had a horse and saddle, a gun, and less than twenty dollars. He also had a woman who believed in him: "I thought my husband was the equal of any man living."

But whereas her father had started out in Oregon with fifty cents and in less than ten years had over twenty thousand dollars, Bethenia's new husband was unable to take hold well enough even to provide her with proper shelter. "Mr. Hill was always ready to go hunting, no matter what work was pressing to be done." The unimproved cabin they had acquired along with their three hundred and sixty acres remained unimproved the first year and, by the coming of winter, rain was pouring in and skunks roamed the kitchen at night. "I was not yet fifteen but, girl as I was, I could but realize that this condition was due not only to poor management, but to a want of industry and perserverance."

At Hill's insistence the couple tried one move after another to improve their situation. First they went back to "visit" Bethenia's father at his ranch near Roseburg where the Owens family had moved to accommodate their growing herds. If her father was surprised that his new son-in-law had given up so quickly on making his own way, he said nothing. Next Hill took his wife to live near his family in the foothills of the Siskyou Mountains. Unlike Bethenia's parents, Hill's apparently refused to help the couple. Having tried to lean upon each set of parents, Hill cast around for some other scheme whereby he could achieve easily what usually comes hard. This time he decided to join the gold rush occurring in Yreka, California.

Although Bethenia was considerably younger than Hill, she had grown up with a sense of strong values and belief in her own abilities. "A girl of fifteen was then considered a woman . . . I was at home in the saddle (on the journey to Yreka) and felt perfect confidence in myself." But her sense of confidence in Hill was dying. He had forced her to sell her two cows in order to finance the will-o'-the-wisp chase to Yreka.

In Yreka Bethenia gave birth to a son whom they named George. As if she had not worries enough about how her husband was failing as a provider, one of Hill's aunts urged her to give up the baby to her: "I will give him all that I have and that is more than his father will ever be able to do for him. I know very well that LeGrand will just fool around all his life and never accomplish anything."

Bethenia was of stronger stuff: "My baby was too precious to give to anyone."

By 1857 the couple was back trying a new start in Roseburg. Bethenia had been sick since childbirth and the baby was ill and fretful. Hill could not stand the baby's condition and treated his callously. Often he lost his temper with both wife and child, as though his own failures were somehow their fault. Finally Bethenia went to her parents and told them she could stand marriage to Hill no longer. Her mother favored a separation, fearing that ". . . with his temper he is liable to kill you at any time." But Bethenia's father told her to go back and try again.

Before long the baby was sick again, and again Hill acted up under strain. Added to her troubles with Hill were Bethenia's anxieties for her child: "I slept little that night, expecting that the child would be in convulsions before morning." This time when she went home to her parents she stayed.

Hill repented of his treatment of Bethenia, but it was too late. Deep within herself she had formed a strength and resolve that was never to leave her in her whole life. Just as Anna Shaw's weak father had forced her to become a strong person, Bethenia's weak husband had forced her to develop a determination to meet life on her own. To her penitent husband she said, "I have told you many times that if we ever did separate, I would never go back, and I never will."

Although she was free after four years of roller-coaster life with Hill, she was in a difficult position: "And now at eighteen years of age, I found myself broken in health and spirit, again in my father's house, from which only four years before I had gone with such a happy heart and such bright hopes for the future. It seemed to me that I should never be happy or strong again . . . surrounded with difficulties seemingly almost insurmountable—a husband for whom I had lost all love and respect, a divorce, the stigma of which would cling to me all my future life, and a sickly babe of two years in my arms, all this rose darkly before me." On top of all this Bethenia could scarcely read or write, having only been to a three-month's school taught by an itinerant teacher the summer she was twelve years old.

"I realized my position fully and resolved to meet it bravely, and do my very best." The first step in her new resolve was to go to school. After getting up each morning at four a.m. to help with the family milking, she went with her younger brothers and sisters to primary school.

After mastering the fundamental subjects she decided to go to live with her married sister and begin to earn her own way. Before leaving her parents' home, however, she filed for a divorce. A neighbor woman, shocked at her action, advised her that the only permissible cause for divorce was adultery. "Go back and beg him on your knees to receive you," the neighbor urged. Bethenia answered firmly, "I was never born to be struck by mortal man."

The divorce blew up into a rough court fight because Hill's mother sought custody of Bethenia's child, hoping thereby to draw her own son closer to her. Bethenia's attorney, later governor of Oregon, fought the case successfully and Bethenia secured her divorce, custody of the child, and the right to resume her maiden name.

The struggle only deepened her determination "to make my own livelihood and that of my child." This she first did by taking in laundry, "one of the few (occupations) considered 'proper' for women in those days." To this she added sewing and nursing and "thus a year passed profitably." But she became restless "because of my intense thirst for learning. An education I must have at whatever cost."

Then in 1860 her chance came. Friends in Oyster, Washington, with whom she was visiting offered to let her stay with them and go to school there. She agreed to their proposal only if she could earn her own way. For the next five years she struggled to get an education, actually spending most of this period in Astoria where she took in laundry, did housekeeping, and finally was teaching school. Before she got this far she had to bear the "humiliation of having to recite with children from eight to fourteen years of age." But she stuck to her studies, beginning each morning at four a.m., and advanced rapidly. "Nothing was permitted to come between me and this, the greatest opportunity of my life."

Not only did she manage to support herself, take care of her son George, and progress in school, but she also managed to save enough money to build herself a little house in Astoria. After her heartbroken disappointment in Hill, she rejoiced greatly in her own ability to do well.

During these five years of working eighteen and more hours a day, Bethenia was "as happy in my independence, I dare say, as John D.

Rockefeller.'' Repeatedly Hill wrote to her asking her to remarry him, but she steadfastly refused. Then one night he showed up in person and found, as Bethenia viewed it, not the child-bride he had abused but ''a full-grown, self-reliant, self-supporting woman who could look upon him only with pity.'' Although Hill had failed to provide child support he asked if he could have George visit him. Bethenia agreed but, being older and wiser, alerted the town sheriff to make sure George was not taken out of town.

In 1867 she returned to Roseburg and started what was to become a successful millinery business. By 1870 she was able to send her son to the University of California at Berkeley. With her easier financial situation there began to grow in her the desire to become a doctor. She borrowed a copy of *Gray's Anatomy* from a friendly practitioner and studied it avidly. S. F. Chadwick, the attorney who had fought her divorce case, heard of her ambition and told her, ''Go ahead. It is in you; let it come out. You will win.''

Systematically she began to make arrangements to go East to medical school, turning over her business to her sister. ''But I was not prepared for the storm of opposition that followed. My family felt that they were disgraced . . . people sneered and laughed derisively.'' One respected woman friend told her that she personally would never have a woman for a doctor. Bethenia choked back tears and replied, ''Time will tell. People have been known to change their minds.''

Against all arguments she set out for the East, taking a train from Marysville, California, on a rain-swept night. She was all alone in the car as the rain beat down and there came to her the full realization ''that I was starting out into an untried world alone, with only my own unaided resources to carry me through.''

Her unaided resources were sufficient. Despite the doubts that assailed her as the train stood in the Marysville station, Bethenia completed the course offered at Philadelphia's Electic School of Medicine.

On her return to Roseburg those male doctors who opposed women in the profession pointedly invited her to attend an autopsy on a male corpse. The doctors and many of the townspeople were shocked when she accepted the invitation. ''Don't you know that the autopsy is on the genital organs,'' one of the doctors said. ''No, ''said Bethenia as she stepped forward to participate,'' but one part of the human body should be as sacred to the physician as another.''

Her boldness so scandalized the town, however, that later she said she believed she had narrowly escaped being tarred and feathered.

Enraged at the attitude among her own townspeople, she decided to move to Portland and there she fitted up her office with electrical and medical baths, the style of medical treatment she had learned in Philadelphia.

Her practice became so successful that she was able to send George to medical school at Willamette University and her sister to Mills College in Oakland, California. During this time she also adopted the daughter of a deceased patient.

Bethenia was not satisfied to be what was then termed a "bath doctor" and she decided "I've done my duty to those depending upon me and now I will treat myself to a full medical course in the old school."

At the age of thirty-eight she entered the University of Michigan Medical College. She received her M.D. in 1880 and supplemented her education with clinical work in Chicago, further postgraduate work, and a tour of European facilities. On her return to Portland in 1881 she specialized in eye and ear diseases. Although her practice soon reached seven thousand dollars per year, a huge sum in those days, few men were among her patients. But the Roseburg woman who said she would never have a woman doctor changed her mind and became one of Bethenia's patients.

Bethenia became active in the women's suffrage movement and in the Oregon State Medical Society and contributed papers and lectures to both organizations. She called these years some of the happiest and most prosperous years of her life. Looking back on her original decision to become a doctor she said, "I can assure you it was no laughing matter then to break through the customs, prejudices, and established rules . . ."

She was not yet done with controversy, however, for in later years her pioneer advocacy of eugenic sterilization brought another storm around her. Nor was she done with family life. In 1884 she married Colonel John Adair, a childhood friend, and adopted two more children: George's son, whose mother had died, and the newborn baby of a patient. In 1887, Dr. Owens-Adair, then forty-seven, gave birth to a daughter but the baby died within a few days.

Upon her marriage to Colonel Adair, Bethenia gave up her city practice and became part-time doctor and part-time farmer. Her active career in public life continued almost up until the time of her death at the age of eighty-six.

One of the proudest moments in her life occurred in 1905 when the Portland Medical Club hosted the American Medical Association at a banquet honoring women physicians. Bethenia noted, "This is the first time in the history of the sessions of the A.M.A. that women have had a distinct recognition . . . It is another instance of the West setting the pace and establishing precedents for the rest of the country to follow."

By one of those coincidences that is eminently satisfying in history, the honored speakers at the banquet included none other than that other pioneer in the professions, Anna Howard Shaw.

In their speeches to the A.M.A. that day neither of the two women could foresee that seventy years later women would still be struggling against discrimination in entering the professions. Instead, their speeches reflected the great hope they had for the pioneer break-throughs they had made. Bethenia said, "I thank God that I have been spared to see this day, when women are acknowledged before the world as the equal of men in medicine and surgery; and, above all, that my own Oregon is in the forefront of this grand forward movement."

Anna Howard Shaw seemed to speak for both of them and for the other women of the frontiers, both geographical and professional: "I have been traveling on the trail all my life. It was the blazing of the first trails that has been the hardest work, and the travelers in them were few for many difficult and lonely years, but the road has widened and straightened, and the travelers in it have increased, until now it has become a broad, smooth highway, in which the untrammeled women of our country, and ultimately of all nations, may freely and gladly walk."

Women of the Farm Frontier

Miriam Davis Colt and Mary Elizabeth Lease

What the farmers ought to do is raise less corn and more hell
Mary Elizabeth Lease

The dark storm-clouds, (to my mind's eye,) are gathering in our horizon, and even now they flap their cold, bat-like wings about my head, causing my heart to tremble with fear. I am so impressed some nights with this feeling, that I sit up in bed for hours, and fairly cringe from some unknown terror.

I tell my husband, "We are a doomed ship; unless we go away, some great calamity will come upon us; and it is on me that the storm will burst with all its dark fury." Sometimes a voice speaks to me in thunder tones, saying, "Rise, rise! flee to the mountains,—narry not in all the plain. Haste away! Destruction's before thee, and sorrow behind;" and, "you never will be a happy family again.". . .

My husband says, "Miriam, don't feel so; I am afraid you will go crazy. I think it is your imaginings, caused by our disappointments and discomforts."

Miriam Davis Colt and her husband came to Kansas in 1856 from their home in Potsdam, New York, where Colt had first tried teaching and then farming. They were ill-prepared for life on the Great Plains, that broad, harsh flatland stretching from Kansas to eastern Colorado. Having come west to join a planned colony of vegetarians that failed to materialize, the Colts found themselves on their own without adequate experience or resources to cope with life on the plains frontier.

Miriam's diary entries give a vivid picture of their dismal situation: "We are 100 miles from a grist-mill, and 50 from a post office . . . The *one plough* is broken. Father started off this morning to go twenty-five miles, down to the Catholic Mission where is the nearest

135

Mary Elizabeth Lease *Photograph Courtesy of Bettman Archives*

blacksmith . . . each one trying all the time to appear cheerful—trying
to make the best of present conditions . . . A cold, drizzling rain. The
prairie wind comes whizzing in. Have hung up an Indian blanket at the
door, but by putting trunks and even stones on to the end that drags,
can hardly make it answer the purpose of a door. It is dark, gloomy,
cheerless, and uncomfortable and cold inside.''

Their ill-constructed log cabin leaked rain and even though the family huddled under five umbrellas, they were soaked through by each storm. The cold earthen floor and the wind that came in through the cracks in the walls added to their misery. Within a couple of months chills and fever afflicted Miriam's children. She began pleading with her husband to return to the East.

> My husband says we shall have an elegant building spot, that he will build a neat little log cabin, and have the cellar so as to open into it from one side; that on the outside it will be a mound, which we can ornament with vines and flowers; that he will get the large flat stones from the creek, that will cleave apart, for walks to the creek and around our cabin; and that he thinks, when we come to get our goods, have our carpets to spread on our rough floors, our nice little stove to cook by, our bedsteads, dishes, and all the necessaries and comforts our boxes contain, together with our books, that we shall be comfortably situated—shall be "squatter sovereigns" indeed. I do not like to hear that voice which whispers, "this never will be;" but still it will whisper.

Miriam's forebodings that threatened her sanity were actually well-founded. The neat little log cabin her husband envisioned was never built. Instead the family grew more debilitated with illness and the hard living conditions and then finally gave up. As they struggled eastward, sick and impoverished, they were literally in a race with death. Miriam's three-year-old son died on the return journey and was buried on the prairie, his headstone reading "Willie the Little Stranger." Colt too died before the family reached the Mississippi. Miriam and her young daughter made it home to New York and there she stayed.

Six years later Miriam published her diary under the title *Went To Kansas*. So grim was its portrayal of life on the plains frontier that it should have served as a deterrent to all but the most hardy and well-equipped.

But within a few years of its publication tens of thousands of would-be settlers flooded across the plains, seeking free land under the 1863 Homestead Act and roused to great expectations by the publicity of the railroads eagerly seeking settlement of the vast empty land that they now served. In less than six years an area greater than the thirteen original colonies was populated and there were scatterings of settlement over an even larger area.

Around these homesteads the great flat plains stretched away without another house or even a tree visible from horizon to horizon. It was the place where, in Western parlance, you could look farther and see less. Miriam Colt had written in her diary, "We are as much shut out here from the world as though we were on some lonely island in the ocean.'' For the lonely women set down in what seemed to be a flat and empty universe, visitors were so rare that one woman said she knew company was coming for dinner if she saw dust rising on the horizon at dawn.

The essential loneliness of women on the plains was captured graphically by a traveler who kept a journal of a train trip through the area:

> The most desolate of these stations is enlivened by the presence of children, not always well-behaved, not always cleanly, but merry and wide awake. At one, however, I saw a woman sitting at the window of her little unshaded house, with her face supported by her hands — a pale, worn despairing face, though youthful, looking out through long locks of spiritless yellow hair at the world going by.

The insanity that Miriam Colt's husband warned her of actually overtook some unknown number of plains farmwomen. Given the living conditions, poverty, hard work and loneliness of their situation, it is surprising that all the women did not go insane or, like Miriam Colt, try to escape the crude existence.

For many of the women the houses made of sod, the sole building material in a treeless land, offered little more than an animal-like cave existence. A description written, not by a fastidious Eastern lady, but by a rugged Pennsylvania farmboy, tells of one of the problems of life in a ''soddie'':

> The people who lived in sod houses, and in fact all who live under a dirt roof are pestered with swarms of bed bugs . . . bugs infect the log and sod chicken coops too in countless thousands, or, if you wish to measure them up in a spoon, you can gather them up that way from between the sods in the walls.

In a soddie dirt trickled constantly into everything — the cookpot, the wash water, the cradle — especially when, as happened periodically, cattle walked on the roof to graze on grass sprouting from the sod. In a heavy rain, the trickles of dirt turned to streams of mud.

Women on the plains were exposed to new experiences even more harrowing than the daily dreariness of life in these earthen, half-buried structures. Prairie fires or cyclones could come with a rush, leaving paths of desolation and death in their wake. Less dangerous but almost as terrifying to the newcomers were the ominous dust storms that began on the plains in the 1860's and grew worse as the settlers stripped away more and more of the grass covering that held the soil.

One observer returned to Nebraska from a trip east in 1880 and met a dust storm head on.

> All day, I was told, the wind had blown nearly a gale. For moments together the almost solid banks of dust had gone slashing along the streets, hiding everything more than ten or fifteen feet away. At six o'clock there had come a strange calm, followed by a new, ominous rumbling . . . I glanced off toward the southward and saw a dense black mass rise up as if the prairies had been ground into fine powder and then spouted out by volcanic force. The mass moved up toward Omaha with terrifying velocity. It hid the sun, and then almost total darkness closed down upon the city.

Taking refuge in a hotel lobby, the writer encountered a woman settler "ghastly white and with eyes of blank horror." What the reaction of a woman alone in a soddie would be to such a spectacle can well be imagined.

Far more destructive than the dust storms were the hordes of grasshoppers that periodically swarmed across the plains. In 1874 plains people were puzzled by the sudden appearance of great silvery circles wheeling through the summer sky.

> Grasshoppers! Inconceivable millions of them! They instantly filled the air. As I shaded my eyes with my hand and looked toward the sun . . . the air seemed filled for a mile upward with flakes of snow. Though the cloud itself passed slowly onward, the ground already was spread with those living creatures — all eating.

The grasshoppers stripped the land bare of every green thing, ate wash on the line, and even attacked leather harness and the handles of tools. Desperately farm families tried to chase off this devastating horde. "They could have fought marauding bands of Cheyennes or Sioux, but these small insects they could not fight." All across the west from Texas to Oregon the pests left swaths of destruction as wide as a hundred miles. In Nebraska the destruction was so complete that serious hunger prevailed and only relief from the East staved off mass starvation.

On this last and cruelest of America's Western frontiers the terrors of nature also included fierce blizzards that swept down from the north, trapping school children far from home and farmers between barn and house. Those caught out in the open commonly lost their way and died. In the blizzard of 1888 which struck in the late afternoon, scores of children died on their way home from school. Stock losses in cattle country the winter of '86 ran between fifty and seventy per cent before the winter broke.

The summer droughts were equally disastrous for the farmers. Basically the plains were a semi-arid region. Their reputation as the Great American Desert up until mid-century was the reason that settlement passed by the huge central plains area until after the Civil War. Then a period of unusually heavy rainfall coincided with the railroads' promotion of the region and the Great American Desert was transformed into the Great American Garden. When the plains reverted to their normal climatic pattern, year after year of drought ensued and crops withered each summer under a blazing sky.

Some of the new settlers endured disaster after disaster and then packed up and headed east with "Went to Kansas and Busted" written on their wagons. Many stayed and hung on grimly to this last chance to acquire free land and a future. Among those who stayed, however, there was a growing bitterness, expressed to some degree in the folk song "Lane County Bachelor":

> *But Hurrah for Lane County, the land of the free,*
> *The home of the grasshopper, bedbug, and flea,*
> *I'll sing her loud praises and boast of her fame*
> *While Starving to death on my government claim.*

The farmers' bitterness was directed not just at the disasters that came from the sky. In fact, those who stayed in spite of grasshoppers, drought and blizzard evolved a considerable body of folk humor and tall tales about the extremes they had experienced. Real bitterness was directed at the railroads, Wall Street investors, and the banks which were perceived to be responsible for the poverty and misery of the plains frontier in the closing decades of the century. The railroads that had lured settlers to the new land so that there might be farm produce for shipping now charged exorbitant rates. Wall Street was blamed for falling prices when grain glutted the markets in the good years; and the banks were hated because of the mortgage foreclosures that followed in the wake of everything else.

By the 1880's the stage was set for rebellion. America's last frontier would close out not with a whimper but a bang. And in the center of this rebellion would be a woman who gave voice and fire to the despair and anger of people from Kansas to Colorado and from Texas to North Dakota.

"Queen Mary," as the plains people came to call her, was born Mary Elizabeth Clyens. In 1870, at the age of twenty, she left her home in Pennsylvania and came to Kansas to teach school. There she met and married Charles Lease, a struggling pharmacist in the prairie settlement called Osage Mission. For a period of ten years the couple tried farming, first in Kansas and then in Texas. During this decade Mary Elizabeth gave birth to four children: Charles, Evelyn Louise, Lena Grace and Ben Hur. In 1883 the Leases' gave up trying to farm in the region and went to Wichita where Lease opened another pharmacy and Mary Elizabeth took in laundry to supplement the meager family income.

Having escaped the loneliness and boredom of the farm Mary Elizabeth took to the urban life of Wichita with zest. In addition to joining various groups and clubs, she began to read law and in 1885 she qualified for the bar.

Meantime she also began a speaking career, her first efforts being on behalf of the Irish National League. She soon identified, however, with the rebellion on the farming frontier that had coalesced into such various political movements as the Union Labor Party, the Farmers' Alliance and, eventually, the dominant Populist Party.

She rapidly became a major figure in the farmers' movement, editing one of its periodicals and addressing a state convention. She was offered the nomination to county school superintendent at a time when women in Kansas were not fully enfranchised, but turned down the nomination in order to keep in the mainstream of what was growing to be the most successful third party movement in American history.

Out on the stump, she was magnetic. "Her magic was in her voice—deep, resonant, and powerful. Her extemporaneous speaking style, charismatic and hypnotic, carried her into such sustained outbursts of emotion and invective that she sometimes could not remember what she had said until she read about it later in the press."

By 1890 with an election in progress in Kansas she hit full stride as a political orator. Across the state of Kansas that year she gave over one hundred and sixty speeches. The countryside across which she moved was aflame with feeling. Recalling those times, one commentator said, "It was a religious revival, a crusade, a pentecost of politics."

It was quite literally the people's movement and they came to rallies, thousands at a time, to hear Mary Lease and others attack the ills that beset them. In one of her speeches, Mary Lease told them:

> Wall Street owns the country. It is no longer a government of the people, by the people, and for the people, but a government of Wall Street, by Wall Street, and for Wall Street. The great common people of this country are slaves . . . Kansas suffers from two great robbers, the Santa Fe Railroad and the loan companies . . .

All through the course of the farming frontier the prices that farmers were paid for their crops had fallen steadily. Hogs and beef that could not be sold for more than two cents a pound were shot by their owners and wheat was burned as fuel. The pioneers on the farm frontier had suffered much to hang on to their holdings in hopes of making a decent living but between 1870 and 1897 crops continued to fall to a fraction of their original market value.

That the area had filled up too rapidly and was "overproducing" in spite of recurring bad crop years was a concept that the Populist movement would not accept. "Overproduction," Mary Elizabeth queried bitterly, "when ten thousand little children, so statistics tell us, starve to death every year in the United States, and over one hundred thousand shop-girls in New York are forced to sell their virtue for the bread their niggardly wages deny them . . . ."

It was at a mass rally in 1890 in Paola, Kansas, that Mary Lease gave the Populist movement its most famous rallying cry: "What the farmers need is to raise less corn and more hell!"

Her colorful speeches and fiery delivery soon made her a major figure in the press. One newspaper misunderstood her name to be "Mary Ellen" and christened her "Mary Yellin" and the name stuck. She was also called "the Pythoness of Kansas" by a press that was largely unfavorable.

Mary Elizabeth and the other Populist leaders scared not only the Eastern establishment that largely controlled the economics of the plains, but also frightened the local businessmen who were concerned with projecting an image of the plains states favorable to business and development. No matter that the conditions Mary and others described were true, these local promoters did not want such harsh facts known nor did they want the area associated with what seemed to them wild-eyed radicals. So eminent a man of good sense as newspaper editor William Allen White ridiculed the Populist candidates and their campaigners in a famous editorial, "What's the Matter with Kansas":

> We all know; yet here we are at it again. We have an old moss-back Jacksonian who snorts and howls because there is a bath-tub in the State House. We are running that old jay for Governor. We have another shabby, wild-eyed, rattlebrained fanatic who has said openly in a dozen speeches that "the rights of the user are paramount to the rights of the owner." We are running him for Chief Justice, so that Capital will come tumbling over itself to get into the State. We have raked the ash-heap of failure in the State and found an old human hoop-skirt who has failed as a business man, who has failed as an editor, who has failed

as a preacher, and we are going to run him for Congressman-at-large. He will help the looks of the Kansas delegation at Washington. Then we have discovered a kid without a law practice and have decided to run him for Attorney-General. Then for fear some hint that the State had become respectable might percolate through the civilized portions of the nation, we have decided to send three or four harpies out lecturing, telling the people that Kansas is raising hell and letting corn go to weeds.

(White later changed his views regarding the movement).

The Populists were not discouraged by such ridicule or opposition, but kept on campaigning through 1890 and subsequent years. By 1891 Mary Elizabeth was carrying the crusade into all the plains states and even into the South, where the Western Populists had hoped to forge an alliance with Southern farmers.

The same spirit that moved Mary Elizabeth and other Populist leaders permeated the ranks of the farm people. A commentator on the period has pointed out: "Mary E. Lease and half a hundred others who lectured up and down the land were not the only people who could talk about the issues of the day . . . The dragon's teeth were sprouting to every corner of the State (of Kansas). Women with skins tanned to parchment by hot winds, with bony hands of toil and clad in faded calico could talk in meeting, and could talk straight to the point."

Though Mary was pre-eminent in the field, numerous other women took an active part in the political movement, clambering up on wagon seats to stand and express their views at the numerous rallies and giving voice to their opinions in a way that women had seldom done before. "Women who never dreamed of becoming public speakers, grew eloquent in their zeal and fervor. Farmers' wives and daughters rose earlier and worked later to gain time to cook picnic dinners, to paint the mottoes on the banners, to practice with the glee clubs, to march in procession." A popular humorist of the day, Josh Billings, surveyed the scene and wrote, "Wimmin is everywhere."

The great campaign brought success at election time. In 1893 the Populists took over the state government of Kansas and made gains in other states. With her party in power, Mary Lease was appointed to head the state's board of charities. The next year, following a disagreement with the governor, she was fired from the job. The following year she published a book called *The Problem of Civilization Solved*. The reforms she suggested ranged from the improbable to the sound, among the latter being establishment of the referendum and initiative processes as ways of giving more direct political power to the people.

In 1896 Mary Elizabeth made a gallant effort to prevent the Populist party from joining with the Democrats in the nomination of William Jennings Bryan. She wanted the party to remain a force in its own right, separate from the two major parties that had so long ignored the plight of the farmers. Bryan had pre-empted many of the Populists' reform goals, and strategists within the Populist movement who wanted fusion of the parties prevailed over Mary Lease in spite of her arguments that fusion meant the disintegration of the organized movement. At the Kansas City convention where she and her supporters made a last effort to stop the endorsement, someone turned out the lights in the convention hall. "It makes a neatly dramatic end," one commentator has written, "to the story of Mary Elizabeth-Ellen Lease, this picture of her yelling from the platform in a futile protest against the darkness inexorably closing in, and it was in fact the end of her career as a national figure."

Enraged by what she considered a sell-out by the Populists, she switched her support to the Republicans and in 1896 campaigned for William McKinley. Thereafter she became a progressive Republican and worked for woman suffrage.

After she went East in 1896 to campaign for McKinley she never returned to the West. In 1902 she divorced her husband and went to live with her son in New York. There she lectured to adult education classes and served for a time as the head of the National Society for Birth Control. She died in 1933 at the age of eighty-three, having lived to see many of the reforms she had worked for become a reality.

As vivid a character as Mary Elizabeth was, she was not the only woman to gain prominent position in the Populist movement. Annie LePorte Diggs, also of Kansas, has been traditionally credited with being one of the principal political organizers of the Populist movement, working behind the scenes quietly while Mary Lease drew the greater public attention. Both were necessary in the functions they performed for the movement but they greatly disliked one another.

Among the other women important in the Populist movement were Sarah Emery of Michigan. She was the first woman ever chosen in the state to be a delegate to a state party convention, in this case the Greenback party, a forerunner of the Populist party. By 1891 she was active in Populism and working in St. Louis as associate editor of the movement's principal journal.

Not to be overlooked among the women who joined the rebellion on the plains is Caroline Arabella Hall, who forced acceptance of women into the previously all-male Grange, the widespread farmers' organization that was also a predecessor of the Populist movement. Caroline Hall traveled from her home in Minnesota to the Grange's headquarters in Washington to argue successfully that women be admitted to the fight. Later she supplied the movement with a songbook which was widely used.

Mary Elizabeth Lease and other women of the Populist movement saw many of their goals become national policy, among them the direct election of senators, the graduated income tax, the control of monopolies and utilities, government control of currency, and regulation of Wall Street practices. Basically, however, the great victory was their bringing to national attention the desperate situation of the plains farmers. Sustained help and the kind of reforms necessary to alleviate the suffering of plains families were a long time coming, but the year Mary Lease died the New Deal with its far-reaching farm programs was only three years away.

"Whether or not this woman was really dangerous," one writer has said of Mary Elizabeth Lease, "men thought she was, and her appearance was an apparition that scared half the country into a somewhat more decent consideration of how painfully the other half lives."

In their efforts Lease and her women associates became the first women to play a major public role in an important American political party and thereby influenced the developing political conscience of the nation.

Willa Cather *Photograph Courtesy of Bettman Archives*

12

Willa Cather

Pioneer of Western Literature

Some memories are better than realities
Willa Cather

In mid-1895 when the prairie summer lay across the land, a young woman stepped aboard an eastbound train to begin a journey away from her Nebraska home and to the world of art and culture. Willa Cather was age twenty-three, and ahead of her lay a long career in which she would pioneer in literature with the same determination and individualism as the pioneers who had broken the Nebraska prairie to the plow when she was a child.

Her future career would encompass successively editorship of the nation's foremost magazine, the authorship of best-selling novels and other works, the winning of the Pulitzer Prize and honorary degrees from the major American universities, and critical recognition as one of the best novelists of her time.

But for Willa Cather and her art what lay ahead was never to be independent of what she was now leaving behind. Through all her life, but especially in her writing, she would always be rooted to the Nebraska prairie land.

She had come here an exile, a child nine years old suddenly removed from the gentle and beloved landscape of Virginia, set down on the raw, treeless prairie of an alien countryside. "I would not know how much a child's life is bound up in the woods and hills and meadows around it, if I had not been jerked away from all these and thrown out into a country as bare as a piece of sheet iron," she wrote thirty years later.

She was an alien among aliens, neighbor to immigrants from Russia, Germany, Norway, France, Sweden—people drawn to a harsh land by

147

the promise that this land at least would be their own.

> Trees were so rare in that country, and they had to make such a hard
> fight to grow, that we used to feel anxious about them, and visit them as
> if they were persons. It must have been the scarcity of detail in that
> tawny landscape that made detail so precious.

With a child's sharp eye she began to find detail in this strange world
where houses "were built of the sod itself, and were only the
unescapable ground in another form." The flat lands broken by sudden
draws; prairie grass "the colour of wine stains"; the
sunflowers—"some of them as big as little trees with great rough
leaves and many branches which bore dozens of blossoms . . . a gold
ribbon across the prairie"—the strange beauty of the prairie became
familiar and loved, etching itself into her deepest being. "By the end
of the first autumn that shaggy grass country had gripped me with a
passion I have never been able to shake."

For a brief while after her family arrived on the plains in 1883, the
Cathers tried farming on the vast grasslands. Alone or with her
younger brothers, Roscoe and Douglas (her sister Jessica was yet a
baby), "Willie" explored the new world, "not a country at all, but the
material out of which countries are made." The children climbed
windmills, dreamed afternoons away by the slow-moving river, and
pridefully killed rattlesnakes.

Willie did something else as well; she came to know intimately the
foreigners whose crude houses, half-hidden in the earth, were scattered
over the vast, forbidding land. Some were of peasant stock but others
were people of education and artistic ability who had brought to the
New World the arts of the Old World. Thus there began for Willa
Cather a duality of being critical in her life and in the development of
American literature. Fused within her was a passionate love for the raw
new land and an equally passionate love of music, drama, and
literature. From exposure to the fragments of culture carried to the
prairies by the exiles of Europe there was implanted in her a restless,
insatiable yearning for art and for the life and satisfactions of the artist.
From the raw land about, devoid of culture and even civilization, came
the materials that would feed her art. Yet between the two elements
there was an essential conflict that she would resolve artistically only
many years later at the height of her powers and in her personal life
would never resolve satisfactorily.

Just over a year after the attempt at farming began, the Cathers gave
it up and moved to the little town of Red Cloud. Only fourteen years

earlier the area had been virgin country, the first settlement at Red Cloud then being a blockhouse built in 1870 against Indian raids. By the time Willie and her family settled into a white, clapboard house rather too small for the growing family, Red Cloud had spurted to a population of over two thousand people with all the vigor of a railroad town in the fast-developing West.

Although the move brought a broader range of life to her sharp attention (many characters in her stories work for railroads), she was in no way separated from the Nebraska countryside. So long as people who knew her were still alive in Red Cloud she was remembered there as a girl on horseback, going where she would. And wherever she went, what she saw remained with her in almost photographic clarity to appear in her later writing.

> July came on with that breathless, brilliant heat which makes the plains of Kansas and Nebraska the best corn country in the world. It seemed as if we could hear the corn growing in the night; under the stars one caught a faint crackling in the dewy, heavy-odoured cornfields where the feathered stalks stood so juicy and green.

> The sky was brilliantly blue, and the sunlight on the glittering white stretches of prairie was almost blinding . . . the whole world was changed by snow . . . the deep arroyo through which Squaw Creek was now only a cleft between snowdrifts — very blue when one looked down into it. The tree-tops that had been gold all the autumn were dwarfed and twisted, as if they would never have any life in them again. The few little cedars, which were so dull and dingy before, now stood out a strong dusky green. The wind had the burning taste of fresh snow; my throat and nostrils smarted as if someone had opened a hartshorn bottle.

The vividness of her descriptive writing is remarkable in its ability to evoke the plains for anyone who has known them. But more remarkable is the fact that such graphic, intensely detailed description was possible to her over twenty years after she left the prairie.

The exploration that Willa Cather conducted in these early years was every bit as important in its own way as the explorations of the trail blazers of the Western frontier. What she was discovering in the prairie land was a vein of material as richly important to American literature and culture as were any of the fabulous Western mines to the economy of the country.

"It was over flat lands like this, stretching out to drink the sun, that the larks sang—and one's heart sang there, too . . . There was a new song in that blue air which had never been sung in the world before.'' Willa Cather would be the first to sing this new song, but her journey to that achievement was to be as difficult in its own way as were the journeys of the pioneers to the West.

Fortunately her family valued books and education. She was taught at home by her grandmother instead of attending the inadequate country school. The course of learning was, however, narrow; there was Latin but not mathematics. When she reached high school there were gaps to be filled. In high school she was a lively personality. She suddenly developed a desire to be a doctor. She plunged into dissecting animals and regularly rode with Red Cloud's doctors on their rounds.

How family and neighbors responded to what was undoubtedly considered eccentric behavior is not precisely known. But Willa Cather felt that the small town was a narrow-minded place. In her later work she would repeatedly portray the young artist as a person fighting to escape the narrowness and scorn of the small town. For her, as for Sinclair Lewis and a number of American writers raised in the country, these ''Main Street'' places would be at one and the same time a wellhead of material and a barrier to the developing self.

As a source of material the little town of Red Cloud reappeared over and over again in her works under a variety of names. It was the microcosm under her sharply focused microscope:

> In little towns, lives roll along so close to one another; loves and hates beat about, their wings almost touching. On the sidewalks along which everyone comes and goes, you must, if you walk abroad at all, at some time pass within a few inches of the man who cheated and betrayed you, or the woman you desire more than anything else in the world. Her skirt brushes against you. You say good-morning and go on.

Willful and determined, with a developing sense of the uniqueness of herself, Willa Cather seems to have been little inhibited by the relentless pressure toward conformity. Much to the horror of her mother, she whacked off her hair to boy's length and went about dressed in whatever pleased her. Even at high school age she was asserting, if awkwardly, a sense of her own style and person. This sense of her own style not only lingered on in her way of dressing all her life but, more importantly, became a key factor in her innovative writing.

If the small town frowned at her shorn head and her cutting up of animals, it was at least in no way stifling to her mental development. ''In Red Cloud she . . . had extraordinary fortune in her teachers. With three of them, all people of remarkable gifts, she remained in touch for many years and one was an intimate friend for life.'' One of the three was ''an ally in Willa Cather's efforts to find an environment in which her mind could grow more freely.''

Outside the school halls she was learning foreign languages, appreciation of music, the history and cultural aspects of Europe, the classic languages and the great works of literature. All this enrichment came from the foreign immigrants of Red Cloud who clung to the vestiges of their cultured lives with the same tenacity that Willa Cather showed in reaching out for this wider world. One of these well-loved neighbors and teachers died with the *Iliad* in his hands moments after Willa left a reading session with him. It was an example, she felt, of someone holding to art literally to the end, a trait that was to become essential in her own make-up.

There was another asset available to Willa Cather even on the raw frontier, one which has disappeared in this later day of television and movies. Thirty-five years after she left Red Cloud she wrote a letter to the *Omaha World-Herald* in which she recalled the wonder of the old touring companies that stopped at Red Cloud's ''opera house'' in the course of touring the frontier places. She remembered that, ''Half a dozen times during each winter, a traveling stock company settled down at the local hotel and thrilled and entertained us for a week.'' The magic of theatre—breaking as it did the long, grim prairie winters—affected her for life. So enamoured of theatre was she that by the time she was a student at the University of Nebraska she had become a ''brilliant, slashing drama critic,'' writing for the *Lincoln Journal*. The key thing was that her love of drama pushed her into professional writing. She found herself in one branch of the arts because of her love for another.

Her career at the University of Nebraska was notable beyond her success as a drama critic. She showed again her independence of spirit (though her hair was now more conventional in style) by studying exactly what she chose to study with little regard for the professors' curriculum.

She was fortunate in what the University of Nebraska was able to offer its students. ''By January 1890 the great period of the University had begun.'' To the potential student the University announced: ''Advantages are offered to all free of charge for tuition, without regard for sex or race or place of residence on the sole condition of possessing the intellectual and moral qualifications requisite for admission to such an invitation.''

At this time, but twenty years after whites and Indians had warred over Nebraska, the school was able to produce not only a Willa Cather but Alvin Johnson, later founder and director of the New School for Social Sciences in New York; scientist Howard Taylor Ricketts; famed orthopedic surgeon Hiram Winnett Orr; poet and philosopher Hartley Burr Alexander; philologist and folklorist Louise Pound and her brother Roscoe Pound, pre-eminent jurist; and writer Dorothy Canfield Fisher. The last three were particular friends of Willa Cather.

During these years the plains states were plunged into severe economic crises. Willa's father had engaged heavily in land investment, and the abandonment of farms to mortgage holders and bank failures nearly ruined him. The family's need for money was the incentive for Willa's entry into journalism, and she began writing her drama column and others.

Pressured for money, exhausted by work at both job and school, and still very uncertain as to where her life and her work really lay Willa Cather was suddenly visited one night in the *Journal* office by a strange figure who brought to her a kind of message of direction.

"He was slender and narrow-chested and wore shabby gray; his soft felt hat was low over his eyes . . . His shoes were dirty, worn about the toes . . ." This wraith-like visitor, who seemingly came out of nowhere, was Stephen Crane, author of the *Red Badge of Courage,* one of America's finest writers, and only two years Willa's senior.

"Quite without invitation on my part (he) began to talk," Willa recalled. Crane spoke at length and with bitterness of the difficulties of the craft of writing: "from the first throb of creative desire . . . to the finished work of the master."

"He spoke slowly and monotonously and even calmly, but I have never known so bitter a heart in any man . . . It was an arraignment of the wages of life."

Crane was caught, as Willa Cather was to be, between writing to live and writing to create. The first kind of writing came easy; the second was agony. Then he said something of the greatest significance to the future art of Willa Cather: "The detail of a thing has to filter through my blood, and then it comes out like a native product, but it takes forever."

Crane''s "forever' was cut short; he died young, much to the loss of American literature. But his odd visit that night as he bummed his way to Mexico meant much to Willa Cather. She took from him something of the fire to be on the move too, to extend her own horizons. She took also from him an understanding of what price the art of a writer would exact. And most of all she took from him that final statement—that art must come from the center of one's being, out of one's very blood "like a native product."

She graduated in 1895 and for a year drifted aimlessly through life in Red Cloud, helping her father salvage his business. Her view of her home was at this time resentful. She felt trapped, lost, and with no future. But her parents to whom she was devoted apparently were anxious for her to deliver the promise she had shown and to evidence some results for her education.

And then her chance came. Friends in Lincoln secured her a job editing a small new magazine in Pittsburgh that was directed at the home-and-hearth market. Thus came the summer day in 1895 when Willa Cather stepped aboard the eastbound train and left Nebraska behind her. She never returned to live in Red Cloud but in a very real sense she never left it. In some way she was ever after frozen psychologically in that last moment before she stepped on board the train and, for her, so was the prairie land.

Over the next years she worked at editing, first for the Pittsburgh magazine and then for a newspaper before shifting to high school teaching. The hack-level work of the first jobs took from her other writing whereas, she believed, school-teaching would not drain her writing talent but would give her more time for her creative work. Up to this point she had had some small success with after-hours work. A number of her stories, articles and poetry had been published, first in a little magazine called *The Library,* then in more noted periodicals—*McClure's Magazine, The Critic, The Criterion, Cosmopolitan* and *The Ladies' Home Journal.*

The struggle to carry two jobs, to support herself and yet be able to write, was compounded by the dreariness of boarding house life. She was not only struggling but lonely. Then she met a young local woman, Isabel McClung, who had read her articles in the Pittsburgh newspaper and before long Willa was a prized member of the McClung household.

Pittsburgh, a place of mills and industry, became for the girl from Red Cloud a center of art and culture, theatre and music. It was mecca to her and she enjoyed to the hilt the pleasures of what was for her the Big City, capped by a trip to Europe with her new friend.

The trip to Europe was a feast for Willa. "The impact of the past touched Willa through her ability to imagine the long-gone time and the people who then lived." Like few writers before or since she would be able later to use this imaginative ability to achieve within her own writing a meaningful relationship between the Old World and the New.

At the end of a decade in industrial Pittsburgh, the antithesis of the open Nebraska plains, Willa Cather published her first book, a collection of short stories entitled *The Troll Garden*. The publisher of the book came to Pittsburgh to meet her, and offered her the editorship of *McClure's Magazine,* a magazine considered of unprecedented stature in American publishing and "the best general magazine ever to be published anywhere."

Thus, in 1906, recognized as a leading literary talent, Willa Cather arrived in New York, the real mecca of her trade, and took over a major position in the field of publishing.

She did astonishingly well. *McClure's Magazine* prospered impressively under her efforts. Circulation increased sixty thousand during her first year and climbed by an even higher figure the next year. McClure's published in bold-face type the announcement that three issues in twelve had sold out of print and that this particular issue was the largest in the magazine's successful history.

Years passed and Willa Cather produced a novel while still at *McClure's*. The novel was competent, of some interest in the early appearance of themes she later used, but it was essentially conventional and of limited value.

The problem was rooted in the demands of her job and the fact that she had not yet found her voice. S.S. McClure, an astute publisher, had recognized Willa Cather's abilities as a writer, but the job was burning her out with exhaustion. And the writing she was doing was not fulfilling her true promise, a promise perceived by Sarah Orne Jewett, literary grand-dame of the period. Jewett's own work is now very dated but to her perceptiveness the world owes in part the development of a talent greater than her own. In the few months that she knew Willa Cather before her death she ceaselessly urged the younger woman to recognize that her work as a writer must be done under less stress, and that it must be out of her unique being, "the native product" as Crane had termed it.

Then in 1912 Willa Cather finally made the step that was to change American literature and place her in the rank of pioneers. It was actually a complex of steps: She left *McClure's;* she produced a story called "The Bohemian Girl," and she went to visit her brother Douglas in Arizona. Most important of all, she began work on a novel called *O Pioneers!* that was to be a milestone in American literature.

With the publication of *O Pioneers!* Willa Cather became the first writer to transmute the American West and the pioneer experience into major literature. "This was the first time I walked off on my own feet—everything before was half real and half an imitation of writers whom I had admired. In this one I hit the home pasture and found that I was Yance Sorensen (a Nebraska neighbor) and not Henry James."

She had found her own voice, the voice to sing a "new song . . . which had never been sung in the world before." With *O Pioneers!*, Willa Cather began in a major way to utilize her Nebraska experience and the Western frontier as the primary materials of her art.

For the first time the West and America's frontier experience became part of a conscious, serious and enduring literature.

Willa Cather was the first writer able to portray Westering as a significant and universal human experience, exploring its contradictions and various levels of meanings with great artistic skill. She was the first to use Western people as major fictional characters and, while preserving their distinctiveness as Westerners, disclose in them what was universally human.

Suddenly, not only had the West found a literary voice but American writing had become authentically American. Hers was the first major work to mark what has been called America's "Coming of Age" in literature, a willingness to deal seriously in literary art with native American materials. Although it was not immediately recognized she had in almost one stroke "shifted the geographical center of literature toward the heart of the continent."

Until her breakthrough critics such as Ezra Pound and H. L. Mencken had clamored in vain for a literature truly related to native American life. Until *O Pioneers!* literature had been defined by the Eastern establishment of that day, the self-conscious literary clique of New York and Boston, frozen in its concern for refinement, for things European, for convention in form and content and for a delicate sensibility. There was little interest in the East in what was seen to be the cultural wasteland of the West, far removed from Europe then dominating America's arts in a way that was actually strangling development of a native American literature.

The movement called for by such as Pound and Mencken would eventually culminate in the great literary decade of the 1920's with such giants as Faulkner, Lewis and Hemingway. But Willa Cather was the first, and the courage it must have taken to "step out on my own feet" was great.

Cather not only introduced an authentic West into major literature but also was the first to create serious literary characters based on the people who had come as immigrants to America from eastern and southern Europe all through the late 1800's and early 1900's. They were an important part of the American scene but had been totally ignored in books except as objects of comedy or derision.

Equally significant, Willa Cather was the first to create in her women characters of substance, capable of carrying the action of the story. Until her novels, women in American literature had almost uniformly been creatures of romance, their dimensions limited by the literary conventions of gentility and sentimentality. Those few women placed in a Western setting in books were the weak sisters and sweethearts in a world of strong Leatherstocking types who were always on hand to rescue the poor creatures. It was also virtually a rule that if a woman was a major character in a novel she was so only as part of a love story.

In contrast, Willa Cather's women were, as critic Carl Van Doren noted, "not the darlings of heroes but heroes themselves." They stride forward from her pages as total people, the strongest of them being self-realized, elemental in strength, and firmly independent.

The gallery of her women characters is rich and varied. Weak or strong, they are interesting people—"Crazy Mary," made insane by the harsh prairie life; the gentle, gaunt aunts and grandmothers who survived the earliest, most terrible pioneer years with dignity and faith; the "lost ladies" who could not find scope for their vivid personalities in the narrow life of prairie towns; and the determined women who broke away to become singers, or writers. There are also the business women—a girl who manages her father's accounts, a domestic who makes a success of dressmaking and reaches the top of her field in San Francisco, her associate who parlays a boarding house in the Klondike into a fortune in gold and real estate.

But perhaps most memorable of all are the earth mother figures, strong and vital women who embrace life, give life, and are at home in the world of the West.

Of these last the most notable is Antonia Shimerda of *My Antonia,* a Bohemian girl who comes to the Nebraska prairie as a child. Her family knows no English and has no skill for life in the new land. Their home is worse than a sod hut, being nothing more than a dirt cave. The hard life embitters her mother, and her gentle father despairs and kills himself. But nothing can overcome Antonia. On the farm as a young woman she plows and works like a man. To get money to educate her younger sister, she becomes a hired girl in town and has a brief time of dances and pretty dresses. Deserted by a lover, she bears a child but goes on living without bitterness. Eventually she marries a poor young farmer, bears ten children and in spite of a hard life of farm work, rejoices in her existence. "It was no wonder that her sons stood tall and straight. She was a rich mine of life, like the founders of early races."

To the feminist of today there may appear to be a conflict inherent in the diverse types of strong, successful women that Willa Cather portrayed. How does one reconcile the values of the earth mother, the business woman, and the artist? There never appeared to be such a conflict for Willa Cather nor for her characters. She seemed content to let each character be, with no self-consciousness of having to satisfy the values of other roles. Indeed, if her depiction was representative of the reality of the times, it would appear that women were psychologically more whole and content on the 19th century frontier than they are in the mid- 20th century urban world.

For Willa Cather herself the choice of roles appears to have been simple. She was exclusively the artist. Although she expressed the belief that art, marriage and motherhood could be combined for others, she believed no such combination was possible for her. She repeatedly stated (though she kept most of her private life and emotions hidden from the public) that art was her only life, totally demanding of her whole self.

In her art she not only rendered the Western scene, experience, and people with great skill; she also drew from the landscape of the West great mythic symbols. The Blue Mesa of the Southwest, a plough seen against the setting sun, a cave in the New Mexico mountains, the prairie grass that grows on a suicide's grave—are transmuted from the physical level to other levels of meaning. Seldom is her symbology obvious; one *senses* the meanings of Cather's symbols rather than experiences them intellectually.

After publication of *O Pioneers!* Cather lived on in New York's Greenwich Village, writing productively for about twenty years. Her life was quiet on the surface, hidden by a passion for privacy and shared with a few close friends and a wide circle of acquaintants in the world of the arts. She made frequent visits to Red Cloud until the deaths of both her parents broke all ties with the small town.

Something else had broken too. She once stated' that "the world broke in half in 1922." The world she saw evolving about her—commercial, automobile-oriented, hurried, devoid of concern for the past—offended her. On the trips home to the prairie she had seen a new softer generation replace the pioneers. Even the trees that she had watched anxiously in their hard fight to grow were being chopped down by a new generation, careless of the meaning of the old struggle for survival, ignorant of what a tree had meant to the pioneers confronted with a land "bare as sheet metal."

The softer life of the new generation had been made possible by the success of the pioneers whom she had admired. Their triumph had been the plowing under of the shaggy grassland that gripped her passionately. She admired their struggle, but their victory meant death of the wild land she loved.

There was for her another conflict—that between the raw New World she loved and the cultural values she prized that were associated with the Old World. In her later novels, *Death Comes For the Archbishop,* and *The Professor's House,* she resolved something of this problem by discovering "the ancestors"—the ancient Indians who had built a civilization of cliff dwellings in the mesa land of the Southwest. More than ever in this day of increased appreciation for mysticism and for the spirituality of the American Indian, along with the deepening desire of many people to be reunited with the natural world, the later works of Willa Cather offer an exploration of that meaning which seems to lie beneath the physical world she described so unforgettably. In this area of the mystical aspects of the American West, she was also a pioneer.

Her life finished quietly in 1947, the intervening years filled with honors and the esteem of the leading artists and intellectuals of her day. Her books were immensely popular both in this country and abroad. In the last ten or fifteen years Willa Cather has been generally neglected; pioneers are commonly forgotten when the ground has been won. William Faulkner, Ernest Hemingway, and Sinclair Lewis (who said he thought she should have had the Nobel Prize he won) over-shadowed her and then a whole new generation came into being oriented to a world in which hers faded like the last faint traces of the old wagon roads. But her books remain, immortalizing those last moments of America's last frontier and the eternal truths she found in those last moments, "persistent human truth repossessed—salvaged, redeemed—by virtue of memory and art."

"Some memories are better than realities," she wrote near the end of *My Antonia,* "and are better than anything that can ever happen to one again."

Notes and Bibliography

The preceding stories are set within the framework of my understanding of the history of the West based upon some twenty years of extensive reading of memoirs, journals, diaries, narrative accounts, letters and other primary sources as well as the standard works of historians and scholars. An accounting of all such sources would be virtually impossible nor does such seem necessary since the overall history of the West presented in this book is generally agreed upon by most authorities.

Where I have attempted to relate the experiences of women to this general history I have, as Willa Cather would say, "walked off on my own feet" and offered my own judgment based principally upon the writings of the women themselves or contemporary accounts. Most of the major interpreters of the Western experience have spent but a page or two on this subject of women in the West. Where I offer my own conclusions or differ with others is indicated either in the text or the notes. This is not to say that others may or may not hold similar views but little has been expressed on the subject. The few works that are an exception are cited under the pertinent chapter.

One work that has been of some overall value and does not fit solely into a chapter category is Dee Brown's *The Gentle Tamers: Women of the Old Wild West* (University of Nebraska Press, Lincoln, 1958. Bison Book 1968.) Mr. Brown's work is a popularized treatment of the subject and is lively, entertaining reading. I do not however concur with the focus, which is implicit in the title, nor the book's emphasis on the bizarre. Also of considerable interest though overly sentimentalized and almost totally lacking in attribution is *Women on the American Frontier* by William W. Fowler, originally published in 1878 and reprinted in 1970, Collectors Editions, Ltd; distributed by Van Nostrand, Reinhold Company, Cincinnati.

Chapter 1: Sacajawea

The narrative account of the Lewis and Clark expedition and of Sacajawea's role is based on the journals of the Corps of Discovery in the following editions:

De Voto, Bernard. *The Journals of Lewis and Clark,* Houghton Mifflin Company, Boston, 1953. Sentry paperback edition also available. A condensed version of the journals highly useful to the general reader and valuable for introduction and notes a pre-eminent Western scholar. Unfortunately De Voto offers little comment on Sacajawea.

Biddle, Nicholas. *The Lewis and Clark Expedition.* Narrative in journal form written by Biddle at the request of Lewis and with the assistance of a member of the party designated by Clark. Based on the original journals and notebooks of the two explorers and several others of the party. First printed in 1814 with Paul Allen as final editor. Reprinted in three volumes in 1961 by J. B. Lippincott Company, Philadelphia and New York.

Thwaites, Reuben Gold. *Original Journals of the Lewis and Clark Expedition.* First scholarly printing of the journals, appearing in 1904-5 and reprinted by Arno Press, New York. Eight volumes.

On the question of Sacajawea's history subsequent to the expedition, Grace Hebard's *Sacajawea: Guide of the Lewis and Clark Expedition* (1932. Reprinted 1967 Arthur H. Clark Company, Glendale, California) is the principle work contending that

Sacajawea died at an old age among her own people. Ms. Hebard's work however includes records of the period (pp. 90-1, 111) which actually argue strongly that Sacajawea died in 1812. Confirmation of this earlier date would appear to come from Clark himself who wrote a list of the party members in about 1828 and noted "Se car ja we au Dead."

Conclusions regarding the motives and conflicts in Sacajawea's life are my own and based on the journal record of her actions.

General material about the Indians has been drawn from many scholarly works. The best summary for the general reader is Dale Morgan's "Opening of the West: Explorers and Mountain Men" in *The Book of the American West,* Jay Monaghan, editor; Julian Messner Inc., New York, 1963. A much more extensive work including specific material on the Lemhi tribe is *The Shoshonis* by Virginia Cole Trenholm and Maurine Carley, University of Oklahoma Press, Norman, 1964.

Chapter 2: Narcissa Whitman

A considerable amount of primary source material on Narcissa Whitman is still in existence in the form of her letters and diaries. A representative cross section of these materials has been printed in *First White Women Over the Rockies,* edited by Clifford Merrill Drury (2 volumes, Arthur H. Clark Company, Glendale, California, 1963). In addition a number of her letters were printed in *Transactions of the Oregon Pioneer Association* between 1891 and 1893 and also appear in *Marcus Whitman, Crusader* by A. B. and Dorothy Hulbert (volume 6 of the Overland to the Pacific Series, Denver, 1936). Copies of her diaries and some of her letters may be found in the Bancroft Library of the University of California at Berkeley, Whitman College, and the Huntington Library in San Marino, California.

Additional sources for the general reader are:

Carey, Charles H. *General History of Oregon,* Binsford and Mort, Publishers, Portland, 1971 (third edition). In addition to material on the Whitmans, includes information on Oregon's progressive laws regarding women's property rights and homestead entitlements.

Drury, Clifford M. *Marcus and Narcissa Whitman,* Arthur H. Clark Company, Glendale, California, 1973. Northwest Historical Series. Two volumes.

———— *Marcus Whitman, M.D.: Pioneer and Martyr.* The Caxton Printers Ltd, Caldwell, Idaho, 1937. Fair amount of material on Narcissa Whitman and an appendix listing then location of all published and unpublished letters.

Jones Nard:*The Great Command,* Little Brown and Company, Boston, 1959. Perceptive study of Narcissa Whitman and other missionary pioneers of Oregon.

Ross, Nancy Wilson. *Farthest Reach: Oregon and Washington,* Alfred A. Knopf, New York, 1941. General history.

———— "Murder at the Place of Rye Grass," *American Heritage,* Vol. 10, August, 1959. Concise summary valuable chiefly for reproduction of paintings and drawings by an artist who visited the Whitmans not long before the massacre.

Chapter 3: Juliet Brier

Source material on the experiences of the Brier family consists principally of interviews published in newspapers long after the event or in brief remininscences authored by members of the family. The most important of these are:

Brier, Juliet. "Our Christmis Amid the Terrors of Death Valley," *San Francisco Call,* December 25, 1898. An interview written in the first person. Reprinted with commentary in Margaret Long's *The Shadow of the Arrow,* The Caxton Printers, Ltd., Caldwell, Idaho, 1941 and 1950.

———— Interview in the *San Francisco Examiner,* February 24, 1901. Reprinted in Long.

Brier, Rev. John Wells. "The Death Valley Party of 1849," *Out West* magazine, March-April, 1903. Also in bound covers, no publisher. Brier was only seven years old at the time of the trek and is vague on dates and locations.

All quotes attributed to the Briers in the chapter are from the above sources.

The Brier family and the heroism of Juliet Brier are mentioned in a number of works by survivors of the Death Valley experience. Among the most notable are:

Manly, William Lewis. *Death Valley in '49.* Most widely available edition is Borden Publishing Company, Los Angeles, 1949. Introduction by Carl I. Wheat. A little known classic of Western trails literature and the personal narrative of one of the West's true heroes.

———— *The Jayhawkers' Oath and Other Sketches,* Warren F. Lewis, Los Angeles, 1949. Edited by Arthur Woodward. Reprint of articles authored by Manly for *The Pioneer,* a weekly newspaper of San Jose, California.

Stephens, Lorenzo Dow. *Life Sketches of a Jayhawker of '49,* Nolta Brothers, San Jose, California, 1916. Interesting though less substantive than Manly's account.

Various logs, diaries, and journals of members of Hunt's train are reproduced in Long, *Shadow of the Arros* and in Leroy and Ann Hafen, *Journals of the Forty-Niners,* Arthur H. Clark Company, Glendale, California, 1954. In addition a collection of Jayhawker material is to be found at the Huntington Library, San Marino, California.

Secondary accounts of the Death Valley story include Long op. cit. and:

Belden, L. Burr. *Death Valley Heroine,* Inland Printing and Engraving Co., San Bernardino, California, 1954. Booklet.

———— *Goodbye, Death Valley,* Death Valley '49ers, Inc. Palm Desert, California, 1956. Booklet.

Edwards, E. I. *The Valley Whose Name Is Death,* San Pasqual Press, Pasadena, California, 1940. Booklet.

Wheat, Carl I. "The Forty-niners in Death Valley," bound reprint from the *Historical Society of Southern California Quarterly,* 1939. Booklet.

———— "Trailing the Forty-niners Through Death Valley," bound reprint of article in

Sierra Club Bulletin, San Francisco, 1939.

Information on Nancy Kelsey, Mary Murphy, Tamsen Donner and Peggy Breen is available to the general reader in the works of George Stewart, foremost historian of the California Trail: *Overland in 1844: The Opening of the California Trail.*

The California Trail: An Epic With Many Heroes, McGraw-Hill Book Company, Inc., New York, 1962. Paperback edition, McGraw-Hill, 1971.

Ordeal By Hunger, originally published in 1936; revised edition, Hougton Mifflin. Paperback: Ace Star Book, New York, 1960.

Also on the Kelseys see John Bidwell's *Echoes of the Past* The Citadel Press, New York, 1962; brief account by one of the leaders of the party.

Chapter 4: Dame Shirley

The most readily available reproduction of the Shirley letters is:

Clappe, Louise Amelia Knapp (Smith). *The Shirley Letters from the California Mines* with introduction and notes by Carl I. Wheat, Alfred A. Knopf, New York 1949 and 1970. Western scholar Wheat discovered the Everett letters and discusses their significance in this edition.

Other printings of the Shirley letters in addition to the rare copies of the *Pioneer* magazine are:

―――― *California in 1851: The Letters of Dame Shirley.* Grabhorn Press, San Francisco, 1933. A Wheat edition before he located the Everett letters.

―――― *Shirley Letters* edited by T. C. Russell and including material by a woman associate of Dame Shirley. Rare item printed in 1922.

The original letters by Everett to Clappe are located in the California State Library in Sacramento along with several notebooks she apparently used in teaching school. Also included in the collection is a copy of a letter by Charles Stoddard to the editor of the *Overland Monthly* asserting that Louise "tried to contribute something original during Harte's engagement but he always snubbed her." Also in the state collection is a letter from Stoddard to Clappe (who was his former teacher) dated 1895 and concluding "God bless you, dear old friend."

The most thorough biographical study of Dame Shirley is Rodman W. Paul's "In Search of Dame Shirley," *Pacific Historical Review* May, 1964. An excellent piece of scholarly detective work.

Additional material includes:

Coughey, John Walton. *Gold Is The Cornerstone,* University of California Press, Berkeley, 1948. Overview of the Gold Rush for the general reader.

Baker, Hugh Sanford Cheney. "History of the Book Trade in California: 1849-59," *California Historical Quarterly,* Vol. 30, Mar-Dec, 1951. Discusses the *Pioneer* magazine and "the Golden Age" of the California book trade.

Jackson, Joseph Henry. *Anybody's Gold: The Story of California's Mining Towns,* D.

Appleton-Century Company Incorporated, New York, 1941. A standard overview of the subject.

Long, Orie William. *Literary Pioneers: Early American Explorers of European Culture,* Russell and Russell Incorporated, Harvard, 1935 and 1963. Examines the influential position of Everett and his brother Edward in political and literary circles.

Paul, Rodman W. *Mining Frontiers of the Far West, 1848-1880,* Holt, Rinehart and Winston, New York, 1963. Technical as well as sociological aspects of the mining frontier.

Royce, Josiah. *California,* Houghton Mifflin Company, Boston and New York, 1886 and 1914. As assistant professor of philosophy at Harvard and a native-born Californian, Royce was one of the first scholars to acknowledge Dame Shirley's contribution.

Shinn, Charles Howard. *Mining Camps: A Study in American Frontier Government,* Alfred A. Knopf, New York, 1948. Examines miners' law and lynchings in more favorable light than that accorded by Dame Shirley.

Walker, Franklin. *San Francisco's Literary Frontier,* Alfred A. Knopf, New York, 1939. Dated but still interesting account of California's early literary circles. Discusses Dame Shirley as one of the ''four most interesting figures of the fifties.'' It is Walker who suggests that Louise Clappe's life in San Francisco was lonely.

The above works that deal with Dame Shirley stress her contribution to Western literature; conclusions about her personal development as a strong, emerging person are my own and are based on her letters.

Chapter 5: Minority Women

The story of Juanita of Downieville is recounted in a number of standard works on California history but is best assessed in terms of race relations in:

Pitt, Leonard. *Decline of the Californios,* University of California Press, Berkeley, California, 1966. Also available in paperback, University of California Press.

Other sources are:

Caughey, John W. ed. *Their Majesties the Mob,* University of Chicago Press, Chicago, 1960. Includes the quote ''the hungriest, craziest, wildest mob'' by an eyewitness to the Juanita lynching.

———— *Gold Is the Cornerstone,* University of California Press, Berkeley, California, 1948. Attempts to give both sides of the story, but concludes ''that act (the lynching), just or unjust, may serve as a line drawn between the early and innocent days . . . and the dawning of the second phase of California's Gold Rush.''

Royce, Josiah. *California,* Houghton Mifflin Company, Boston and New York, 1886 and 1914. California's first native-born intellectual condemns the Juanita incident.

Shinn, Charles Howard. *Mining Camps: A Study in American Frontier Government,* Alfred A. Knopf, New York, 1948. Study of the evolution of self-government and lynch law in the Gold Rush camps.

A great deal of material on white attitudes towards people of color in California's early days is to be found in Hubert Howe Bancroft's *The History of California,* The History Publishing Co., Publishers; San Francisco, 1890. Another rich source of material on this subject is the files of court cases of the period to be found in the archives of the various California counties and in the State of California Archives in Sacramento.

An extensive treatment of frontier attitudes toward Indian women, much of which is applicable to other women of color, is in Page Smiths' *Daughters of the Promised Land,* Little Brown and Company, Boston, 1970. Also available in paperback edition.

The principle sources for material on Biddy Mason are newspaper articles and documents of the period reprinted in Delilah L. Beasley's *The Negro Trail Blazers of California,* originally published in Los Angeles in 1919 and reprinted in 1969 by R and E Research Associates, San Francisco. See also Kenneth G. Goode's California's *Black Pioneers,* McNally and Loftin, Publishers; Santa Barbara, California, 1974. Biddy Mason is also mentioned in Loren W. Katz' *The Black West,* a popularized treatment, (Doubleday and Company Inc., Garden City, New York, 1971).

Also of interest are:

Franklin, John Hope. *From Slavery to Freedom,* Alfred A. Knopf, New York, 1967. Though principally concerned with the movement of slaves into the Old Frontier, the chapters on "The Westward March" and "Quasi-Free Negroes" provide background material applicable to the Far West Frontier.

Franklin, William E. "The Archy Case: The California Supreme Court Refuses to Free a Slave," *Pacific Historical Review,* XXXII, 1963.

Lapp, Rudolph. "The Negro in Gold Rush California," *Journal of Negro History,* Vol. XLIX, April, 1964.

The story of Donaldina Cameron is based chiefly on:

File of newspaper clippings, magazine articles, and miscellany concerning Donaldina Cameron in the Special Collections Room, San Francisco Public Library.

Wilson, Carol. *Chinatown Quest: The Life Adventures of Donaldina Cameron,* Stanford University Press, 1931. Also in revised paperback edition as *Chinatown Quest: One Hundred Years of Donaldina Cameron,* California Historical Society, San Francisco, 1974. Based primarily on interviews with Donaldina but vague on dates and chronology.

To be published in 1976 but still in manuscript form at the time of this writing is Mildred Martin's *Chinatown's Angry Angel,* Pacific Press, San Francisco. A more chronological account than the Wilson treatment, utilizing records of the Presbyterian church as well as interviews with people who knew Cameron.

The quotes on the life of Chinese slave girls are from Stephen Longstreet's *The Wilder Shore* (Doubleday and Company, Inc. Garden City, New York, 1968) and consist primarily of newspaper accounts of the period. See also *Nell Kimball: Her Life as an American Madam* edited by the same author (Macmillan, New York, 1970).

Additional material on the general subject is to be found in *Chinese at Home and Abroad; Together with the Report of the Special Committee of the Board of Supervisors,* San Francisco, 1885.

Chapter 6: Winning the Vote

Materials on Esther Morris and Wyoming are from:

Catt, Carrie Chapman and Nettie Rogers Shuler. *Woman Suffrage and Politics: The Inner Story of the Suffrage Movement.* New York. Charles Scribner Sons. 1923.

Dunn, Nora G. "Reminiscences of Fourscore Years and Eight," *Annals of Wyoming,* XIX, 1947. Describes political activity of women in Wyoming after enfranchisement.

Hebard, Grace R. "The First Woman Jury," *Journal of American History,* VII, No. IV 1913.

Morton, Katharine A. "A Historical Review of Woman Suffrage," *Annals of Wyoming,* XII, 1940.

See also the biographical sketch of Esther Morris in *Notable American Woman: 1607-1950,* The Belknap Press of Harvard University Press, Cambridge, 1971. Includes portions of a rare interview with Esther Morris from the *Laramie Sentinel,* January 21, 1871.

Nye, Bill. "Bill Nye's Experience: Tells What He Knows About Woman Suffrage," *Annals of Wyoming,* XVI, 1947. Includes quote on suffrage being "unqualified success." Willard, Frances. "Mrs. Esther Morris" in *A Woman of the Century,* published in 1893 and reprinted as *American Women,* Gale Research Co., Detroit, 1974.

The quoted material on the first woman jury is principally from Morton, op.cit. as is the quote from the *South Pass News* commending Esther Morris' work as justice of the peace and the quote: "Tremendous publicity . . ." The comment that ". . . the real victory passed almost unnoticed . . ." is from *Remember the Ladies,* edited by Carol George (Syracuse University Press, 1975).

The acceptance of the statue of Esther Morris for Washington's Statuary Hall is recorded in Senate Document no. 69, United States 86th Congress, First Session, U.S. Government Printing Office, 1961.

Information on the suffrage career of Carrie Chapman Catt and the history of the woman's suffrage movement is found in:

Catt, op.cit.

Adams, Mildred, *The Right to Be People,* J. B. Lippincott, Philadelphia and New York, 1967.

Flexner, Eleanor. *Century of Struggle,* Harvard University Press, Cambridge, 1959.

Park, Maud Wood. *Front Door Lobby,* edited by Edna Lamprey, Beacon Press, Boston, 1960.

Stanton, Elizabeth Cady, et al. eds. *History of Woman Suffrage,* originally published in 1881 and reprinted in 1971, Collectors Editions distributed by Van Nostrand Reinhold Company, Cincinnati.

Shaw, Anna. *The Story of a Pioneer,* Harper and Brothers Publishers, New York, 1915.

Conclusions about the unique political perspicacity of Morris and Catt are my own, based upon their records of achievement and evaluated in terms of my ten years of active political campaigning.

Chapter 7: Ann Eliza Young

The story of Ann Eliza Young is almost entirely from her autobiography *Wife No. 19 or the Story of a Life in Bondage,* Dustin, Gilman and Co., Hartford, Connecticut, 1875. Reprinted in 1972 by Arno Press, New York.

Ann Eliza's version of life in Mormon polygamy is supported by Fanny (Mrs. T. B. H.) Stenhouse in her autobiographical *Tell It All: The Story of a Life's Experiences in Mormonism* with an introduction by Harriet Beecher Stowe (A. D. Worthington and Company, Hartford; Louis Lloyd and Company, Chicago; A. L. Bancroft and Company, San Francisco; 1874).

Some additional material on Ann Eliza Young is to be found in Irving Wallace's *Twenty-Seventh Wife,* Simon and Schuster, Inc., New York, 1961 (paperback edition available, New American Library, New York, 1971).

One of the best accounts of the Mormon experience for the general reader is Wallace Stegner's *The Gathering of Zion: The Story of the Mormon Trail,* McGraw-Hill Book Company, New York, 1964, American Trail Series and in paperback edition by McGraw.

The assertion that European women were literally trapped into polygamy is my own and is based on the fact that, even after Brigham Young's public announcement of the doctrine in 1852, Mormon missionaries abroad spoke little of the practice. One has only to consider the poverty of the European emigrants and the isolated position of Salt Lake to realize that women who once arrived there were almost totally dependent on their new community and had little hope of relocating outside Mormondom. A check of the rolls of the handcart companies (see LeRoy and Ann Hufen, *Handcarts to Zion,* Arthur H. Clark Company; Glendale, California, 1969) shows a disproportionate number of unattached women, among them a sizable number of widows with small children.

An informal account of life in polygamous families is Paul Bailey's *Polygamy Was Better Than Monotony,* Ballantine Books, New York, 1972. In spite of the title, the author records the ''bitterness'' of grandmothers who had been plural wives.

Chapter 8: Bright Eyes

The most complete work on Susette La Flesche is Dorothy Clark Wilson's *Bright Eyes: The Story of Susette La Flesche, an Omaha Indian,* McGraw-Hill Book Company, New York, 1974. Based in large part upon La Flesche family papers at the Nebraska State Historical Society, the book is unfortunately marred by a great deal of fictionalized conversation and lack of precise attribution.

More readable is Thomas Tibbles' autobiographical *Buckskin and Blanket Days,* University of Nebraska Press, Lincoln, 1969 (Bison paperback books). A lively account of the writer's tumultuous career with considerable material on Bright Eyes and the Ponca-Omaha struggle.

For further reading:

Brown, Dee. *Bury My Heart At Wounded Knee,* Holt, Rinehard, and Winston; New York, 1970. Also available in paperback as a Bantam book. Vivid account of "Indian history of the American West" from 1860-90. Includes a chapter "Standing Bear Becomes a Person" on the Ponca suit but does not mention Bright Eyes.

Mails, Thomas E. *The Mystic Warriors of the Plains,* Doubleday and Company, New York, 1972. Profusely illustrated study of the culture of the Plains Indians including the Omahas and Poncas. Organized by cultural subject rather than by tribe.

Jackson, Helen Hunt. *Century of Dishonor.* Originally published in 1888 and reprinted in many editions in past decade. Pioneering expose of maltreatment of the Indians, inspired by Jackson's association with Bright Eyes and Tibbles. See also the romantic novel *Ramona,* available in many editions including paperback.

The Sheridan quote is attributed to him as taking place at Fort Cobb in January, 1869.

Chapter 9: Women of the Cattle Frontier

The material on Agnes Morley Cleaveland is from her autobiographical *No Life For A Lady,* Houghton Mifflin Company, Boston, 1941.

The story of Ella Watson is best presented in Helena Huntington Smith's *War on the Powder River,* an impassioned account of the notorious Johnson County cattle war (University of Nebraska Press, Lincoln, 1967). Additional reading on Ella Watson is Harry Sinclair's *Notorious Ladies of the Frontier,* also a principle source for material on Elizabeth Taylor. A highly informal and personal evocation of the Powder River Country is Burt Struthers' *Powder River: Let 'er Buck* (Rinehart and Company Inc., New York, 1938, eighth printing 1959).

For further reading on Pamela Mason, see William Ransom Hogan's "Pamela Mann: Texas Frontierswoman," *Southwest Review,* 1935; contains a number of other Mann anecdotes as well as the material here quoted.

The quotations from Sarah Lippincott are to be found in her *New Life in New Lands,* J. B. Ford Publisher, New York, 1871.

Material on the early days of rodeo and women's participation is to be found in Foghorn Clancy's *My Fifty Years in Rodeo,* (Naylor Company, San Antonio, 1952). *The Settlers' West* (Martin F. Schmitt and Dee Brown, Bonanza Books, New York, 1955) contains a brief treatment on the subject and includes photos of some of the early women rodeo stars.

Recommended for general reading on the cattle frontier are:

Abbott, E. C. ("Teddy Blue") and Helena Huntington Smith. *We Pointed Them North,* originally published 1955 and reissued in 1972 by the University of Oklahoma Press, Norman.

Adams, Andy. *Log of a Cowboy,* first published 1903, many reprints including Houghton Mifflin Company, New York, 1955.

Atherton, Lewis. *Cattle Kings,* Indiana University Press, Bloomington, 1961, and Bison paperback, University of Nebraska Press, Lincoln, 1972.

Branch, Douglas. *The Cowboy and His Interpreters,* Cooper Square Publishing Inc., New York, 1961.

Everett, Dick. *Vanguards of the Frontier,* University of Nebraska Press, Lincoln, 1941; Bison paperback, 1965 with fourth printing, 1974.

Dobie, J. Frank. *Cow People,* Little, Brown and Company, Boston, 1964. Interviews with old-timers; introduction ranks Cleaveland's *No Life For A Lady* along with Andy Adam's *Log of a Cowboy* as the only books in which "cow people come to life."

Frantz, Joe B. and Julian Ernest. *The American Cowboy: The Myth and the Reality,* University of Oklahoma Press, Norman, 1955.

Lea, Tom. *The King Ranch,* Little, Brown and Company, Boston, 1957.

Sandoz, Mari. *The Cattlemen,* Hastings House, Publishers, New York, 1958.

Webb, Walter Prescott. *The Great Plains,* Grossett and Dunlap paperback, New York, 1957.

Chapter 10: Professional Women

The stories of the lives of Anna Shaw and Bethenia Owens-Adair are taken from their autobiographies *The Story of a Pioneer,* (Harper and Brothers Publishers, New York, 1915) and *Dr. Owens-Adair: Some of Her Life Experiences* (Mann and Beach, Portland, Oregon; 1906).

Background information on the status of women in the field of work is to be found in:

Brown, Dee. *The Gentle Tamers,* University of Nebraska Press Bison Book, Lincoln, 1968 reprint of 1958 edition. Chapter "Casting Off The Shackles" is a brief survey of some of the more colorful occupations attempted by women of the West.

Hahn, Emily. *Once Upon a Pedestal,* Thomas Crowell Company, New York, 1974. Good overview of the changing status of women in America, contrasting patterns in the East and West.

Ross, Ishbel. *Sons of Adam, Daughters of Eve: The Role of Women in American History,* Harper and Row, Publishers, New York, 1969.

Stern, Madeline B. *We The Women,* Shulte Publishing Co., New York, 1963. Examples of women who were first into various business and professional fields.

Chapter 11: On the Farm Frontier

The story of Miriam Davis Colt is from her autobiographical *Went to Kansas,* originally published in 1802 and reprinted by University Microfilms, March of America Facsimile Series, 1966.

Material on the conditions faced by the plains settlers and on the rise of populism is principally from:

Hicks, John D. *The Populist Revolt: A History of the Farmers' Alliance and the

Peoples' Party, University of Nebraska Press Minnesota, 1931. Reissued as a paperback Bison Book by the University of Nebraska Press, 1961. Excellent scholarly work.

Tindall, George B. *A Populist Reader,* Harper and Row, New York, 1966, Harper Torchbook paperback. Unfortunately does not include any speeches by Mary Lease.

Sandoz, Mari. *Love Song to the Plains,* Harper and Brothers, New York, 1961.

Schmidt, Martin F. and Dee Brown. *The Settlers' West,* Bonanza Books, New York, 1955. Entertaining; many interesting photos. Miller, Nyle H., Edgar Langsdorf and Robert W. Richmond. *Kansas in Newspapers,* Kansas State Historical Society, Topeka, 1963. Facsimile reprint of pages of Kansas newspapers; includes a letter by Mary Lease, stories on the winter of 1885-86, description of sod house, discussion of the "American Desert," etc. Annotated.

The quoted description of the "most desolate of these stations" is from Sarah Lippincott's *New Life in New Lands* (J. B. Ford, New York, 1871.)

Quoted material on the Omaha dust storm and the plague of grasshoppers is from Thomas Tibbles' autobiographical *Buckskin and Blanket Days.* University of Nebraska Press, Lincoln, 1969. "Lame County Bachelor," a folk song popular in 1862 is to be found in many folk song collections.

Material quoted on Mary Lease is principally from Hicks, op.cit. as is the Josh Billings statement, "Wimmen is everywhere." The quote on Mary Lease's . . . "neatly dramatic end . . ." is from Gerald Johnson's *The Lunatic Fringe,* originally published in 1957 and reprinted in 1973 by Greenwood Press, Westport, Conn., a not too flattering portrait of "Queen Mary."

The quote "Her magic was in her voice . . ." is from an article on Mary Lease by Ross E. Paulson in *Notable American Women,* Edward T. James et. al. editors, Harvard University Press, Cambridge, 1971. 4 volumes.

Chapter 12: Willa Cather

A valuable source of biographical information is Mildred Bennett's *The World of Willa Cather,* (University of Nebraska Press, Lincoln; revised edition 1961). Utilizes a number of unpublished Cather letters and interviews with inhabitants of Red Cloud who knew Cather and her family. Unfortunately the book is not well organized. Also of interest biographically is Edith Lewis' *Willa Cather: Living a Personal Record* (Alfred A. Knopf, New York, 1953), by Cather's companion of later years.

A most valuable single source of critical material is *Willa Cather and Her Critics* edited by James Schroeter (Cornell University Press, Ithaca, 1967). A compilation of Cather criticism ranging over a forty year period and including commentary by H. L. Mencken, Edmund Wilson, Joseph Wood Krutch, Rebecca West, Lionel Trilling and a particularly perceptive essay by Carl Van Doren. Not only useful in terms of the work of Willa Cather but an interesting survey in literary commentary.

Other materials that have been useful include:

Allen, Walter. *The Urgent West: The American Dream and Modern Man.* E. P. Dutton and Company, New York, 1969.

Auchincloss, Louis. *Pioneers and Caretakers,* University of Minnesota, Minneapolis, 1961. Cather and others discussed in terms of traditionalism.

Brown, E. K. *Willa Cather: A Critical Biography* (completed by Leon Edel), Alfred A. Knopf, New York, 1953. A standard in the field.

Brown, Marion and Ruth Crone. *Willa Cather: The Woman and Her Works,* Charles Scribner's Sons. N.Y., 1970.

Daiches, David. *Willa Cather: A Critical Introduction,* originally published in 1951 and reprinted in 1971 by Greenwood Press; Westport, Connecticut.

McFarland, Dorothy Tuck. *Willa Cather,* Frederick Ungar Publishing Company, New York, 1972. "A reconsideration of a major American writer."

Morgan, H. Wayne. *Writers in Transition,* Hill and Wang, New York, 1963. See chapter "Willa Cather: The Writer's Quest."

Sandoz, Mari. *Love Song to the Plains,* Harper and Brothers, New York, 1961. Good informal background reading on the area and its history.

Smith, Henry Nash. *Virgin Land: The American West as Symbol and Myth,* Vintage Books, 1950. Reissued 1970 by Harvard University Press. Although it does not specifically deal with Cather's work, the book sets forth the concept of my three symbols relative the the various phases of American consciousness.

Stegner, Wallace ed. *The American Novel from James Fenimore Cooper to William Faulkner,* Basic Books Inc., New York, 1965. Essays by outstanding American writers and critics including "Willa Cather: My Antonia" by the editor.

Thorp, Willard. *American Writing in the 20th Century,* Harvard University Press, Cambridge, 1960.

Van Ghent, Dorothy. *Willa Cather* University of Minnesota Press, Minneapolis, 1964.

Of special interest is *Willa Cather: A Pictorial Memoir* by Bernice Slote and Lucia Woods (University of Nebraska Press, Lincoln, 1973), a beautiful array of photos of Cather country coupled with quotes from her work.

Of Willa Cather's novels, particularly recommended are *O Pioneers, My Antonia, The Professor's House,* and *Death Comes for the Archbishop,* all available in a number of editions.

All quoted material is from Cather's own statements or fiction except:

E. K. Brown (op.cit.) "In Red Cloud she . . . had extraordinary fortune in her teachers . . ."

Marion Brown: "The impact of the past touched Willa . . ."

Sandoz: various quotes on the University of Nebraska

Schroeter ". . . shifted the geographical center of literature . . ."

Van Ghent: ". . . persistent human truths repossessed . . ."

INDEX